Advanced Fusing Techniques

GLASS FUSING BOOK TWO

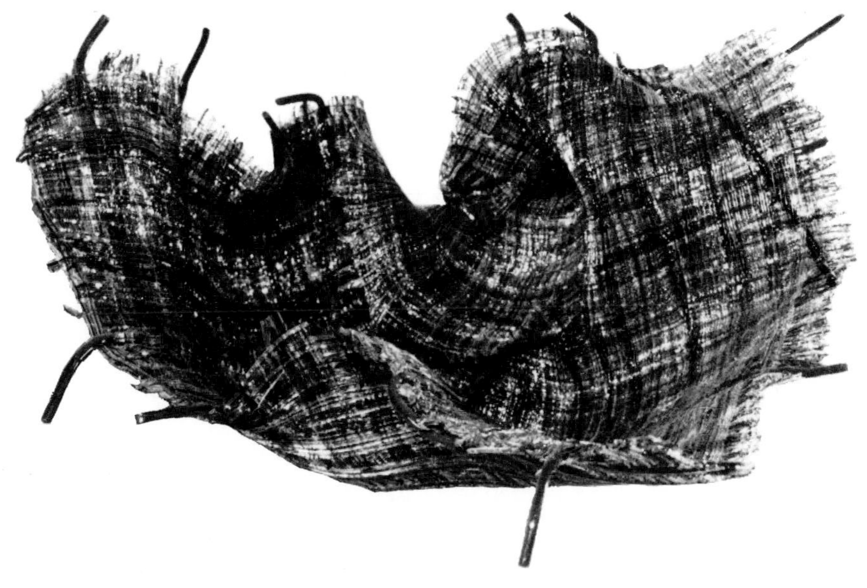

Written by

BOYCE LUNDSTROM

Published by

VITREOUS PUBLICATIONS

Published by Vitreous Group/Camp Colton

Second Printing 1991

Library of Congress Catalog Card Number 83-50657

ISBN Number 0-9612282-1-0

Edited by Kathleen Lundstrom

Designed by Linda Andrews

Photography by Joan Malone, Linda Andrews and Boyce Lundstrom.

(Cover) Stringer Fabric by Dan Ott.

(Title Page) Stringer Bowl by Dan Ott.

Table of Contents

I have been very fortunate in having a wonderful group of past students and teaching associates work with me on this book. We gathered together for a few wintry weeks at Camp Colton and punished the studio, attempting to re-demonstrate everything I would write about. You will see their sometimes smiling, sometimes goofy, always dedicated faces, as you progress through these pages. And you will see their art.

Ruth Brockmann, Dan Ott, and Peter Wendel have taught with me for many years. They are excellent teachers, as well as fine artists, and they know the material glass thoroughly. They helped so much by being great communicators. Ruth maintains her glass studio in Seattle, Washington, Peter his in Corvallis, Oregon, and Dan is presently living and working full time at Camp Colton.

Doug Pomeroy has been a teaching assistant at Camp Colton and has a voracious appetite for experimentation. Doug lives for glass and is one of the quickest studies I've ever known of any new process. He maintains his studio in Corvallis, Oregon.

Mike Dupille, Seattle, Washington and Linda Andrews, Kennewick, Washington, both come from a commercial graphic art background, and both have recently been infected with glass madness. Linda helped with the photography, has redone all of the illustrations, and generously agreed to do the layout art and design for the book. Both Mike and Linda have great talent and will undoubtedly make glass work their entire livelihood in the near future.

Michael Barton, whose art work in glass has always been among of the most unique and most unsung of that of any of my art glass friends, is a studio commission artist in Sacramento, California. Michael's quiet participation and unique vision was a refreshing contribution.

Joan Malone, who is newly trying her hand at glass art, provided much of the photography, while Mike Malone gave his time, tools, and knowhow in preparing and maintaining experimental equipment. Joan and Mike have a glass studio in Bellingham, Washington.

So here is a special thanks and an open invitation to come back when the snow falls and the icicles grow on the steep banks of Canyon Creek to:

Ruth Brockmann	Peter Wendel
Michael Barton	Dan Ott
Linda Andrews	Mike Dupille
Joan Malone	Doug Pomeroy
Mike Malone	

Others who helped did not join our wonderful, whacky, winter session. Robert "Do-glass" Ross constructed the first prototype glory hole, as well as drawing the initial breakaway illustrations. Dan Schwoerer who, as always, lent his support for more information for fusers, provided the technical paper on use of Bullseye glass. Many others sent me up-to-date information on how the processes they had learned at Camp Colton were working in their personal studios. And many artists provided photos of their work, included herein. Thank you all.

A special thanks to my wife, Kathy, who pummelled me until the job was done well, or corrected my mistakes and said little. Kathy made this book readable; she found form in chaos, and she keyboarded 100% of the material into the Mac.

Thanks a thousand times everyone and thanks a million Kathy!

Introduction

When *Glass Fusing Book One* was completed (and the title chosen), I must have assumed that I'd write another book on glass fusing. But I don't think that I ever anticipated the scope of the myriad ways we are working with kiln fired glass today. I know I didn't suspect that I would move with my family to Camp Colton and begin to receive a joyous parade of student guests from all over the country, all eager to explore glass processes.

It is those students, all that they have learned, all that they have taught me, and all that they have pushed me to discover, who have been the inspiration for this book. Their delight in the material glass, their unique vision of what they want to make glass do and, yes, their tireless questions have inspired this work.

Each year, at Camp Colton, we share our home and working studio for a few months with students-in-residence, who come to study glass fusing and its many correlary techniques. Consequently, the studio has become a testing ground for equipment, for ideas, and for materials. We have the luxury, together, of taking the attitude that if you wonder about it, try it.

This book is written simply and organized with illustrations and photographs to complement the text. It is about ideas and glass processes. It was written for people who are involved with the material glass. It does assume a basic knowledge of the glass fusing process. Hopefully, each chapter will be only a starting point. When a personal artistic vision is executed in glass, with one's own hands, the resulting object becomes the motivation to continue creating with glass.

Glass is a material that holds the potential to reflect subtleties that the artist put into the work. Through watching students relate to glass and the many processes entailed, I have come to realize that my involvement with glass can be a metaphor for the way I relate to life.

As the seasons pass and more things are wondered about and tried, I find successive groups of students moving more rapidly toward more and more adventurous ways of handling glass. The enthusiasm with which they insisted that it was time for a Book Two has gone a long way in helping me recommit to this project.

It is my hope that you will find some of the answers you have been seeking in the information in this book, but mostly that you'll use this information as a "jumping off" point. As you use the book, you'll be a participant in causing it to become outdated as quickly as the volumes before it, for as things are tried, new things are discovered, new materials invented, and so...

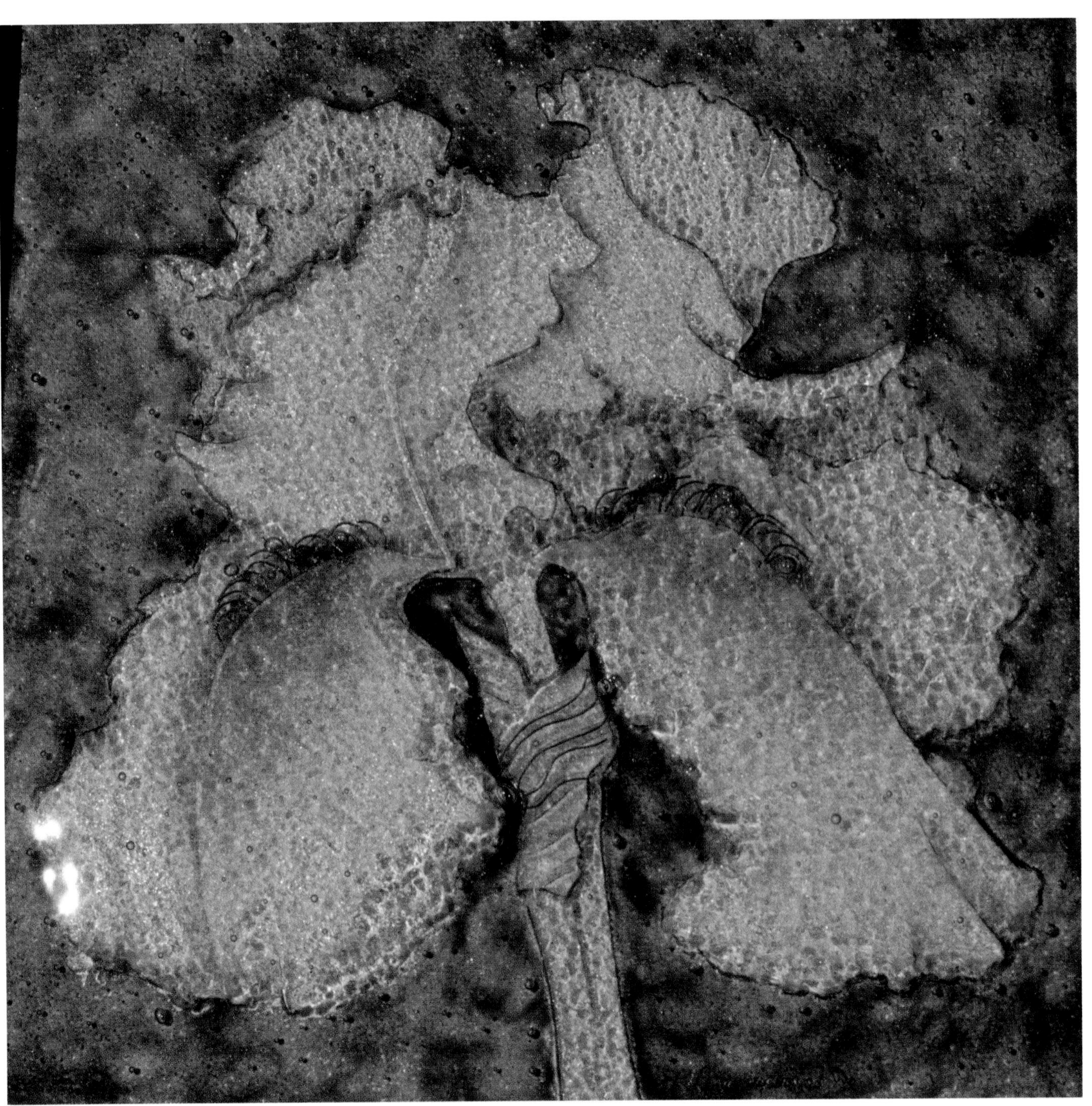

FIBER PAPER RELIEF MOLDS

Probably the simplest, most direct mold material used for glass is fiber paper. Fiber paper, sometimes called fiber felt, is made with alumina silicate fibers held together with an organic binder. The fiber paper can be purchased in 1/32", 1/16" and 1/8" thicknesses and from 24 to 48 inches wide, in rolls of 50 to 100 feet, from industrial suppliers, or in smaller amounts from a glass craft supplier.

The alumina fiber paper can be cut with a razor knife or scissors, torn or pulled apart for an irregular, soft edge, or dye cut for multiples of the same pattern. It has one relatively smooth side and one textured side, either of which may be used next to the glass surface.

Fiber paper can be used to create an image in relief on the surface of the glass. This effect is achieved by laying up or stacking cut pieces of fiber paper on a kiln shelf, then placing a light cathedral or a clear glass over the design and fusing to 1500° F. The glass melts over the fiber design creating thick and thin areas that refract the light differently, creating an image seeming to emanate from within the finished piece of glass.

The fiber paper may be layered up to 1/4" thick if two one eighth inch glass blanks are used to cover the fiber design. This could be four thicknesses of 1/16" fiber or two layers of 1/8" fiber. If the fiber design is thicker than the glass placed over it, the glass will thin so much during firing, in the highest raised areas, that bubbles may form.

Opposite page: "Iris", 12" x 12", Linda Ellis Andrews.

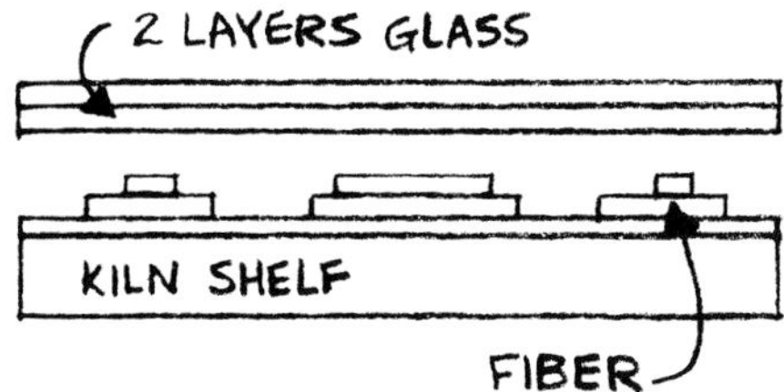

Fiber construction used to create bas relief design in glass. Made of fiber paper, fiber blanket, and fiber board, hardened with colloidal alumina and held together with white glue.

Fiber paper, which is white to begin with, turns dark gray as the temperature of the kiln reaches 500°F, when binders begin burning off. There will be a sweet burnt smell to the vapors, and though not toxic, the vapors should be vented from the kiln and the room ventilated. The fumes will not affect the glass and, by the time the kiln reaches 800°F, the binders have burned off and the fiber paper is white again.

As the firing continues, the glass slumps over the fiber design. At approximately 1350°F the glass has touched the shelf around the outside, closing off the escape channels for air trapped within the fiber. As the glass becomes softer and the air within the fiber gets hotter, this trapped air expands up to eight times in volume, creating bubbles in thin areas. There are three ways to keep this from happening.

If the fiber design is large enough to extend outward past the edge of the overlaying glass blank, interconnecting parts of the design will create a channel for the expanding air to evacuate at the side of the piece. By placing the fiber design on a full sheet of fiber instead of directly on a prepared kiln shelf, the air can escape through the fiber base. The third precaution to prevent unwanted bubble formation is to fire slowly after the kiln temperature has reached 1350°F, and don't fire hotter than necessary for the glass. The maximum temperature for Bullseye and Kokomo cathedrals is 1500°F. For window glass and DeSag the temperature should not exceed 1570°F. By not allowing the glass to get too soft too fast, the air trapped within the fiber paper will be forced out the edges between the glass and the shelf. Spaces between the design elements should exceed 1/4" if the fiber is more than one layer thick. Otherwise the glass will not fill the void without a long, hot soak at maximum temperature.

There is no limit to the thickness of the fiber paper stack, as long as there is enough glass volume covering the design and a sufficient dam to keep the glass from flowing off the shelf. A strip of fiber paper, with the ends stapled together to form a ring, set around the fiber design will keep glass up to 1/2" thick from flowing away from the design. Another way to make a dam

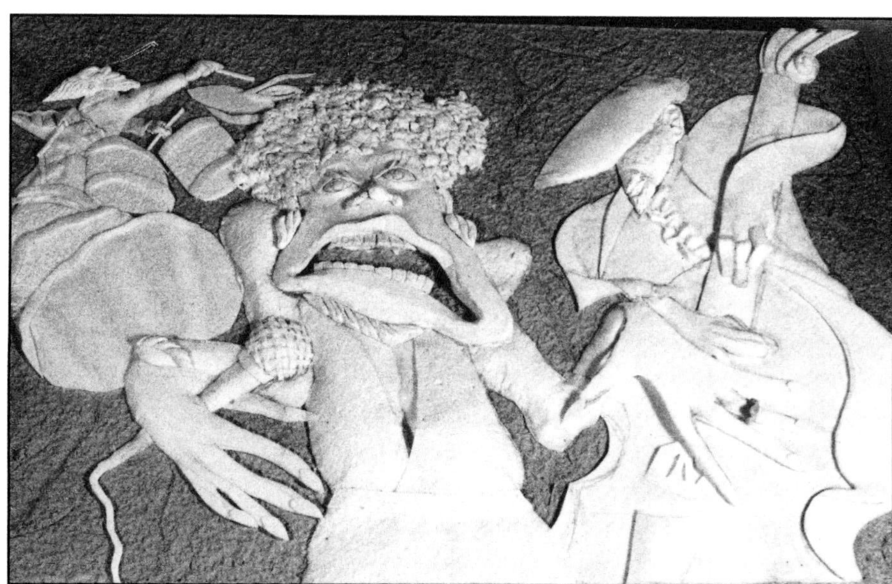

"Small Band, Big Sound", 29" x 40" bas relief tile in clear glass by Michael Dupille, with fiber materials still in place.

is with fiber strips held in place around the design with brick, metal or other refractory material.

Any glass may be fused over the fiber paper. One layer of 1/8" glass will not take on the fiber design as completely as two layers, or 1/4" of glass. One layer will start to contract at 1450°F, before completing a full impression of the fiber design.

Fiber paper molds used with clear or cathedral glass result in an effect where the imagery, when the piece is seen in light, appears to come from within the piece. When opaque glass, dark cathedrals or iridescent glass is used, the glass reflects surface lights, and the effect is quite different.

Fusing over fiber requires longer annealing than simple fusing. The kiln should not be crash cooled. The fiber paper is an insulating material and since the fiber design is not of uniform thickness throughout, some areas will cool faster than others. If the glass is annealed at the same rate as an equal thickness of glass without fiber, differential cooling will set up a thermal gradient within the glass, causing permanent strain or cracking. The general rule of thumb is: anneal for the thickest area of glass, including the thickness of the fiber mold.

After a piece is fully fused on a flat surface and annealed, the fiber paper can be removed and used over again. The fiber is softer and more fragile than it was before firing, and care must be taken in removing it from the glass. Without any additional treatment fiber paper can be used two or three times.

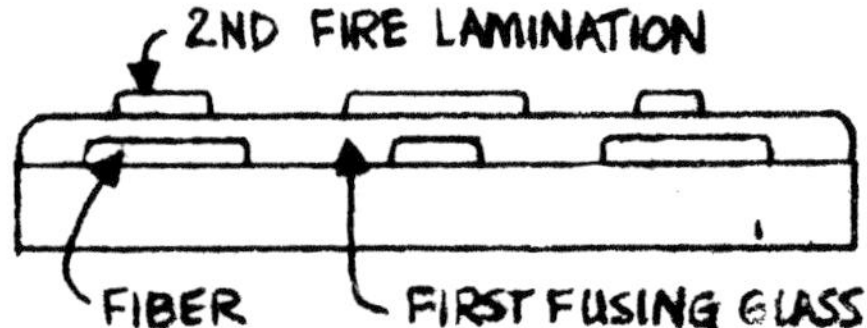

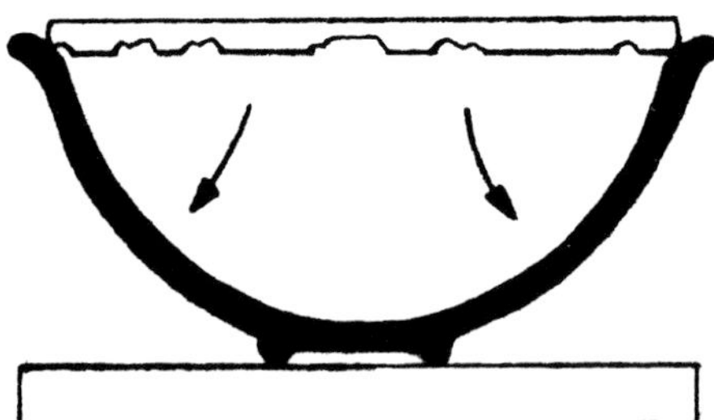

If the intent is to reuse the fiber design more than twice, the following procedure should be used:

1. Fire the cut fibèr design to 1000°F to remove the binder.
2. Spray the fiber design with liberal amounts of colloidal alumina or colloidal silica (fiber mold hardener).
3. Fire the mold a second time to 800°F.
4. Coat the surface of the mold with shelf primer or mold release.
5. Place the glass over the prepared fiber design.

The relief design formed when fusing clear or light cathedral glass over fiber will be retained during a slump firing when the textured area is placed down in the slump mold and fired to 1300°F then held at that temperature until the mold is filled. A long, slow slump will be the most effective in retaining the fiber relief design.

To create an air bubble design within a glass piece, place the textured side down on top of another glass blank before slumping. This will trap air in all the areas where glass doesn't touch glass (or laminate). The design will soften and some of the detail will be lost. This process allows control and repetition of bubble patterns.

A variation of this process is to fill in the design on the textured side with transparent enamels and fire, face up, to 1200°F. Then, in a third firing, laminate the textured, enameled glass blank to another piece of glass. If this is not done in two separate firings, the gases given off by the enamels will cause irregular bubbling and loss of design.

An added texture or a third dimension can be overlayed on a fiber textured piece if the fiber is not removed before the second firing. After firing to 1500°F, anneal and cool the kiln, but do not remove the glass from the shelf. Add small pieces or strips of glass to the top surface, creating a shadow effect to the design formed out of fiber. Fire a second time to 1300°F to laminate this layer, but do not fuse it flat into the surface. The result, after cooling and removing the fiber, will be a piece with a distinct third layer, adding greatly to the light refractive qualities.

Fiber paper is great just as a surface to fuse on. The binder may affect the glass by giving it a foggy or matte surface when using fiber paper as a glass separator (shelf primer) without pre-firing it. Preparing a shelf can be as

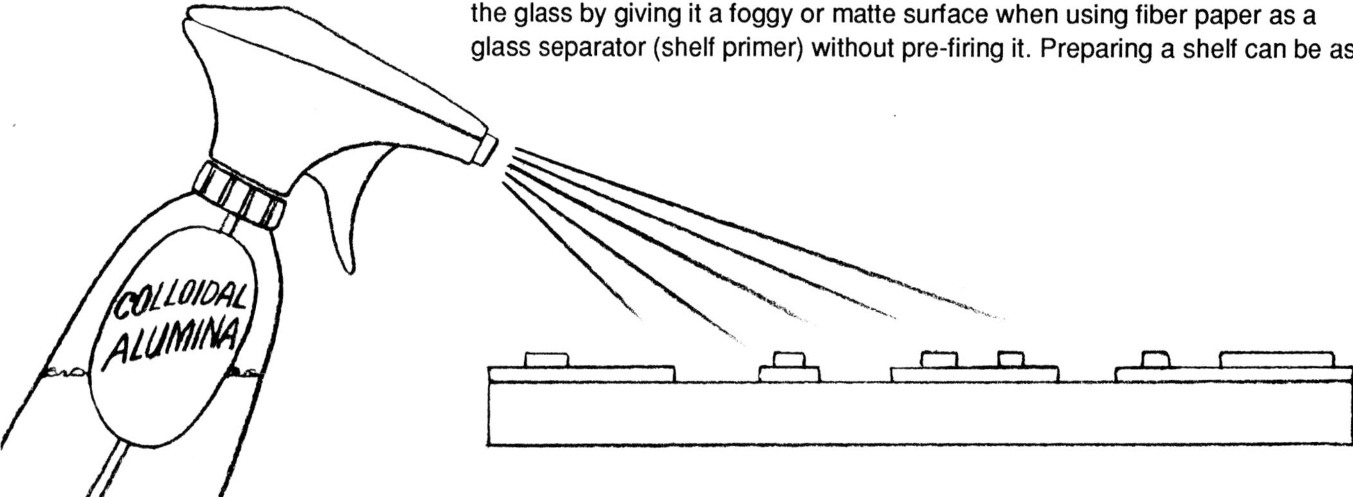

quick as cutting a piece of fiber paper the same size as the shelf. It is important to understand that when an insulating material is placed on a shelf it should be done evenly, to avoid causing the shelf to thermal shock. If only half of the shelf is insulated with fiber paper, the uncovered half of the shelf will cool faster. The resulting thermal gradient can cause the shelf to break. If four 8" X 8" projects are placed on fiber paper on a 20" X 20" shelf and they are layed out in an even pattern, shelf cracking should not occur.

Fiber paper used as a kiln shelf treatment will allow any air between the bottom glass blank and the shelf to escape. This can be the solution to a common problem when firing a top fired fusing kiln and building designs on a large bottom glass blank. In that situation, the edges slump flat against the shelf early in the firing, causing any air under the blank to move to the center. As this trapped air heats it expands and causes large bubbles in the center area of the fused piece.

Fiber has one side that is more textured than the other. The rough side is an excellent texture for tiles that are to remain flat and be grouted or glued to another surface. This pebble-grained surface allows air passageways so that silicon seal or other adhesive will dry thoroughly when tiles are installed. The texture also gives added surface area to which grout can adhere.

"Chuckanut View", glass landscape, made by fiber relief process, Linda Ellis Andrews.

1/8" fiber paper, showing the difference in texture on opposite sides and the effect on edges of cutting and tearing.

Fiber paper scraps and used fiber should be saved to use in plaster molds to add tensile strength. A paste of two parts pre-fired fiber paper, one part silica flour, and one part shelf primer mixed with enough mold hardener to make a paste can be used to fill cracks between contiguous kiln shelves to form a large fusing surface. Apply the paste to clean shelves, free of shelf primer, and fire to 500° F. Cool and sand flat. Cover the entire area with 1/8" fiber paper and prepare the fiber paper as for multiple use (previously explained in this chapter). This is the best way of achieving a large fusing surface without the expense of large shelves, not to mention their inherent problems of shelf warp and heat retention.

Fiber paper is a very versatile material. It can be worked with directly to make a mold to fuse over, or for building a dam to keep the glass from flowing. Fiber paper is the simplest material to add to your studio work because it doesn't require other tools or special skills to use. It can be formed by hand; it can be torn, cut with household scissors, or machine cut with great precision. Because it is made from a long fiber and is very refractory, it has the ability to add tensile strength to other mold materials. The smallest scraps are usable and reusable up to seven or eight times, if care is used.

The fact that fiber paper insulates is at times a drawback of using the material, but even this aspect can be used to advantage. It is relatively inexpensive and is available in varying thicknesses and sizes. Fiber paper is safe to use as long as normal studio safety standards are observed. Wear a face mask to avoid breathing airborne particles of fiber paper that are loosened in the process of sanding or chopping the material. Clean hands before smoking or eating after handling the material.

CALCIUM CARBONATE PASTE RELIEF

Calcium carbonate mixed with water will form a paste. It can then be extruded through a kitchen pastry tube or cake decorator directly onto a prepared kiln shelf to create a raised design. After drying for five to ten minutes, the calcium carbonate becomes firm enough to support two layers of glass placed over the design. When fired to fusing temperatures, the glass slumps over the raised design creating thick and thin areas that reflect light differently, with results much like those discussed under fiber paper mold.

Calcium carbonate paste allows more painterly strokes in the design than is possible with a line cut in fiber paper. The process is quick and the material allows for spontaneity. It goes down on the fusing surface as a rounded line, with a slight undercut at its base. Therefore, the light refractive qualities of the glass formed over the calcium carbonate paste line are different than those achieved when fiber paper is used.

When mixing calcium carbonate and water, add the calcium carbonate powder to the water by sifting or sprinkling it over the surface of the water. Continue to add the powder until the calcium carbonate starts to float on the surface, then wait two or three minutes and let the material slake before starting to mix by hand with a whisk or spatula. Mix small batches that can be used in one or two hours. Left sitting, the calcium carbonate paste will start to set or firm up. It is easier to mix a new batch than to try to thin an old one.

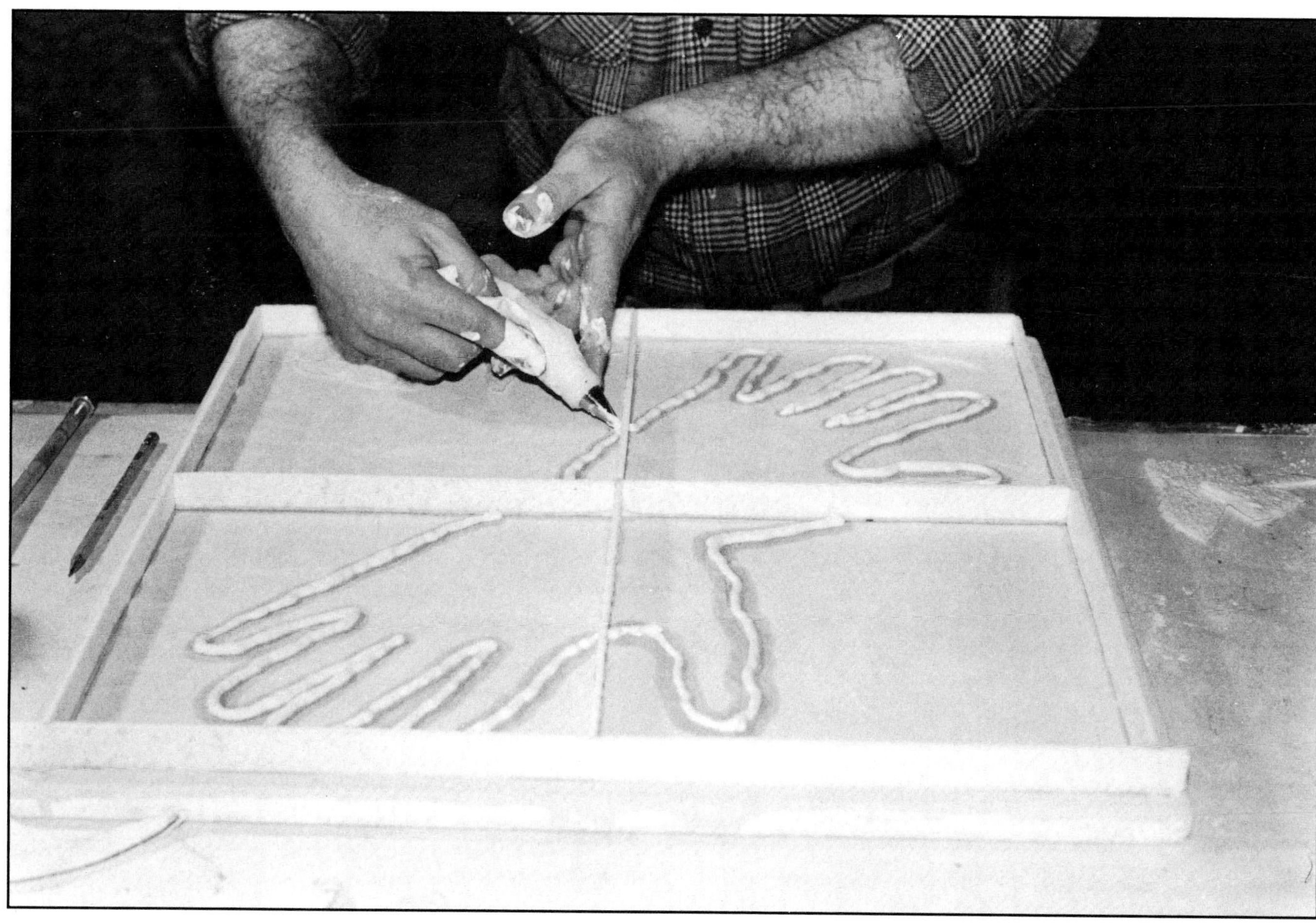

Application of calcium carbonate paste with a pastry bag directly onto a prepared kiln shelf. Fiber dam will separate the glass into four tiles.

Detail view of calcium carbonate paste and fiber paper used together.

Calcium carbonate powder that has been stored in an open container or in a moist place gets small lumps of material that are difficult to dissolve. These lumps get stuck in the opening of the applicator, making it hard to lay out a continuous line. If you find your calcium carbonate has gotten lumpy, replace it with fresh product rather than trying to have success with the lumpy material.

When applying calcium carbonate paste to a dry primered shelf, the shelf quickly absorbs some of the moisture. Within a few minutes the paste is dry enough to remove unwanted lines and reapply the paste where mistakes have been made.

Calcium carbonate paste is often used in conjunction with fiber paper, since the two processes are similar. The paste does not dry as fast when applied on top of fiber, because the fiber does not absorb the moisture from the paste. Air drying can take up to one hour before calcium carbonate will support the glass blank. This can be speeded up by kiln drying, but it should be done at a low temperature, approximately 200 to 250° F, to avoid excessive shrinking and cracking of the paste.

There are limits to how thickly you can apply calcium carbonate paste, whereas there are no limits to how high you can stack fiber. When applying more than one layer, let the first application dry completely, then apply a second coat. The thicker the paste the more it will shrink and crack destroying the design.

During firing, moisture from the paste will evacuate from between the glass blank and the shelf. As the firing continues, the glass slumps over the line design and the calcium carbonate gets totally surrounded by glass. It is at this point in the firing, approximately 1400°F, that the combined water starts to release from the paste. If these gases can escape by following the design to the outside of the form, they will not cause unwanted bubbles. The same techniques for avoiding bubbles apply as when working with fiber paper, the most important being to fire slowly. If the glass does not get soft enough to allow the gases to push through the surface, and if the overlaying glass is thick enough (enough volume), the expanding air will force itself out the sides.

There are different grades of calcium carbonate, which is also referred to as whiting and lime. Ceramic grade calcium carbonate is probably the most consistent and contains the fewest impurities.

Some glasses get a foggy or etched surface where they touch the paste, This is caused by a reaction between the sodium in the glass and the calcium carbonate. High firing temperatures and extended contact of glass with the paste increase the risk of fogginess. After firing, the calcium carbonate can be cleaned out of the design with water and/or Zud and a fine wire brush.

The finished bas relief mold ready for glass. Each of the four tiles is 10" x 10", so the entire layout fits on 20" kiln shelf.

"Day Meets Night", Michael Dupille.

Do not put your finished product in water until it has cooled to room temperature. A very small amount of retained heat can cause thermal shock because the glass varies so radically from thick to thin.

Dolomite ($CaMgCo3$) can be substituted for calcium carbonate (whiting). Dolomite also frosts the surface of most glasses but is much easier to remove from fine detail after firing.

Calcium carbonate paste is a great mold material, allowing freedom of expression in design. It is easy to control and permits varied line quality. Fast strokes with a medium-sized, round tip produce a wide to narrow line, very

much like a brush stroke. Calcium carbonate paste may be applied with a brush or a pallet knife or it can be press molded and placed into design forms. In combination with fiber paper it adds fine detail, a different line quality and the ability to create quick, expressive drawings. It is so inexpensive that projects designed on the shelf can be scraped off and discarded, then redone until the artist is satisfied with the result.

CARVING CASTIBLES FOR BAS-RELIEF

Fiber paper and calcium carbonate paste are additive processes for building up bas-relief designs. Carving away material is a subtractive process and is often preferred by many artists who come to glass from other media where they have experience in carving. Carving plasters also offers the ideal surface for achieving fine detail and texture variation as well as variation in depth of relief.

The requirements of a good carving castable are that it be porous enough that trapped air will exit through the plaster material, that it's surface doesn't harden too rapidly, and that it has a fine grained texture and stays consistently firm, but not hard over an extended period of time. Molding plaster and No. 1 pottery plaster work well. White art plaster and No. 1 casting plaster contain materials that make the surface harder and are not recommended, but will work if that is all that is available.

To minimize the shrinkage of the plaster at elevated temperatures (over 1200° F) it is necessary to add a refractory filler. Silica or diatomatious earth (a filtering agent that can be obtained at swimming pool supply shops) should be added to the plaster in quantities of 50% by weight. Since diatomatious earth is light weight, 50% by weight will equal approximately 70% by volume. The addition of these fillers make the plaster shrink less at high temperatures and give the mix a smooth carving texture over a two or three day period. This is very important when carving a large area.

Pieces of glass are held in place on the relief design by a dam supported by the kiln walls.

Bas relief mold of carved plaster-composition.

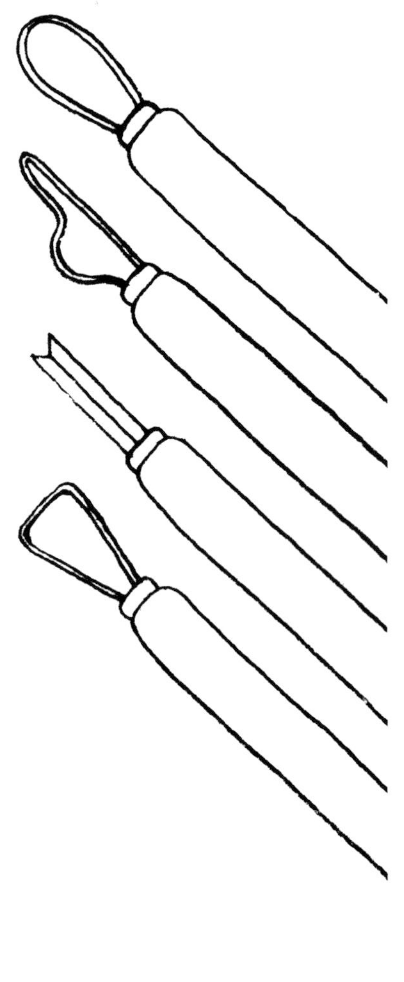

THE PROCESS

The plaster and silica mix are added to cold water in the usual way but should be mixed with a jiffy mixer for an extended time: 5 minutes for small batches (3 to 7 pounds) and longer for larger batches. This will cause the plaster to form smaller crystals upon hardening and decrease the burnout shrinkage. The plaster is then poured onto a kiln shelf that has been covered with 1/16" of fiber paper. Wide masking tape stretched around the outside shelf edge will act as a dam. Remember to level the shelf so that the cast plaster slab will have an even thickness. After approximately three hours the plaster will have a carving consistency that will remain the same for two to three days if covered with plastic when not carving.

Ceramic carving tools with wire loops in one of a number of shapes, fastened to wood handles, work very well for carving plaster. Scrapers, knives and ice picks all impart their individual texture or line quality. The surface can be smoothed with a wet, fine-grained sponge. Heavy relief, up to 5/8", can be carved into a one-inch slab. Be sure to leave approximately 1/2 of the thickness of the plaster slab depth intact to keep cracks from forming when the plaster does shrink. The thin fiber paper will keep the plaster mix from adhering to the shelf and will allow it to shrink evenly.

A carved slab 20" by 20" should be allowed to air dry for two days before it is placed in the kiln. Dry the carving for five to ten hours at 250°F, then raise the temperature gradually over three hours to 1200°F for final curing. Cool the carving by natural kiln cooling; it can crack if cooled too fast. If large cracks do appear, the carving can be repaired with additions of the same mix applied with a brush. At this point the carving has shrunk approximately 1/4" to 3/8" over the 20" length. It will shrink a little more when fired to 1500°F, but not enough to result in fisures into which the glass can run.

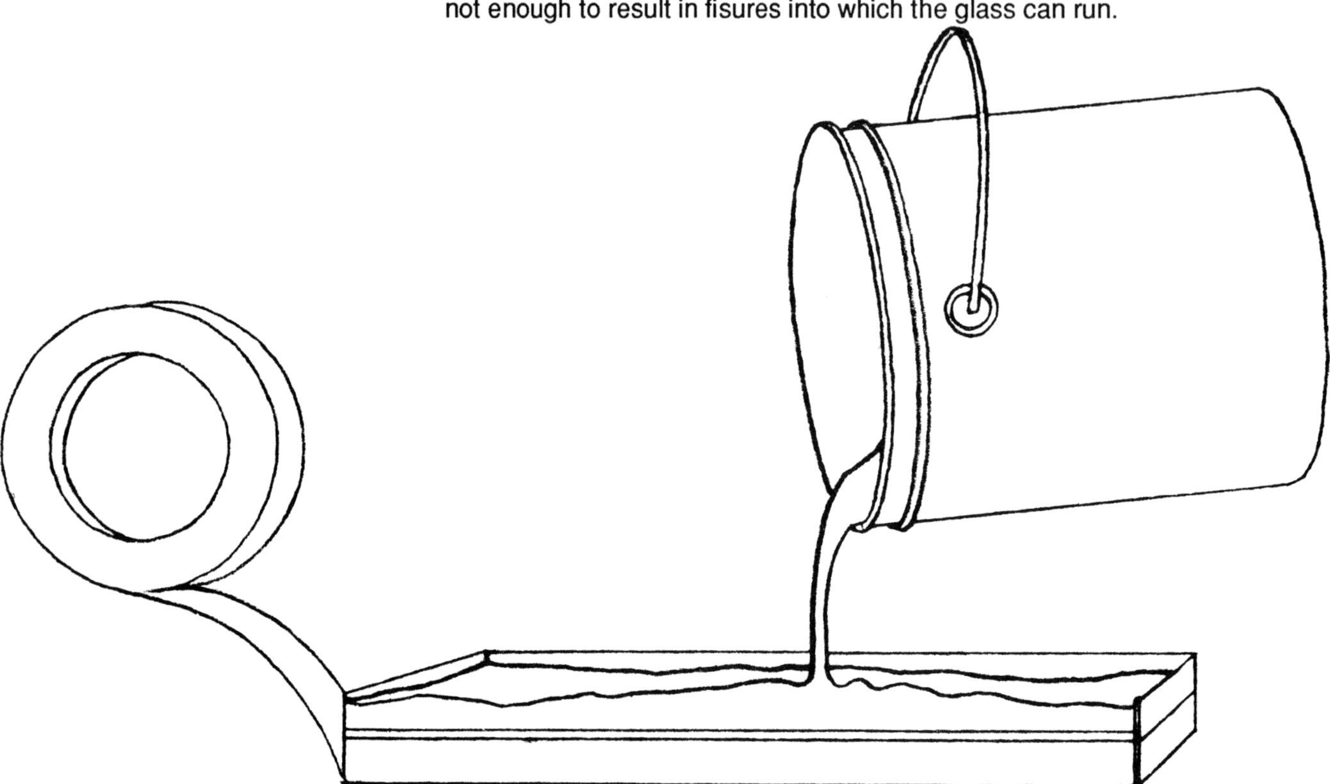

Glass will not stick to the plaster mix and no separator is needed. If more than one impression is to be taken from the relief mold, spray the surface with a liberal amount of colloidal alumina or mold hardener after curing and firing to 1200° F, and fire again to 500° F. This will make the surface more durable and not as much detail will be lost when the first glass fusing is removed.

"Flowering Universe", Michael Dupille.

Plaster silica castable mold, after the first fused impression has been removed. A second impression can be taken after cracks are filled with powdered, used mold material.

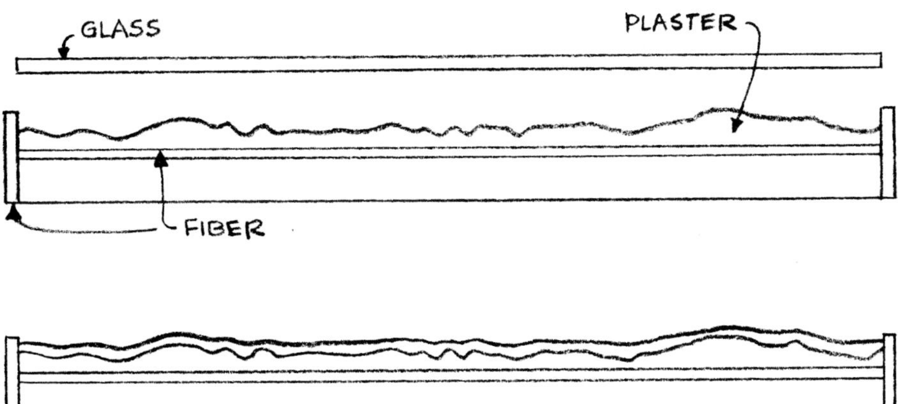

The amount of glass to be placed over the carved mold depends on the intended results. At least two layers of 1/8" glass are recommended if fine details are to be picked up, and three layers if the depth varies up to 1/2". Full sized sheets will give the most accurate representation of the carving. Smaller cut pieces often show the division lines when back lit. When using two full sized sheets and firing to 1500° F, bubbles may be apparent when the piece is back lit. Fuse the sheets flat to 1600° F, letting the bubbles rise to the surface and pop them. Slump and texture fuse over the plaster mold and the result will be a homogenous large textured fusing with no apparent bubbles.

Bas Relief

There are many possible ways of applying glass to a flat, textured mold. Iridized glass fused with the iridescent side down (against the mold) will give surface reflected light so that many facets reflecting from the iridization can be seen from all angles. A layer of clear glass covering an opal glass will add a visual depth to low areas that makes the design seem deeper that it actually is. Frit may be used exclusively over the entire surface of the mold, filling in the low areas with light cathedral colors and shading toward the surface with clear frit. When filling a bas-relief mold with frit, cut the plaster slab one inch smaller than the supporting shelf before carving, and make a dam with fiber paper supported with strips cut from kiln shelves. Different firing temperatures used to consolidate the frit will give dynamically different results.

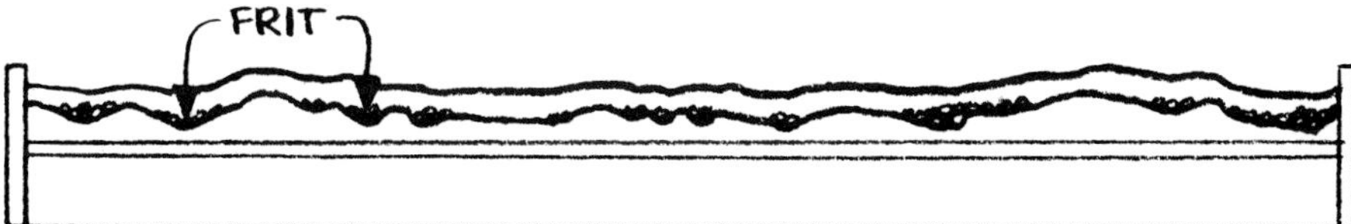

Firing temperatures and annealing schedules for bas-relief molding techniques depend on the amount of glass used. For example, one layer of glass can be slumped over a simple relief mold of up to 3/4" variation in depth, forming wavy patterns, but not picking up fine detail without thinning so much in raised area as to become so fragile that it will break. Therefore, one layer of glass should be fired to 1400°F and allowed to soak at that temperature for thirty minutes. Two layers can be fired to 1550°F and soaked at that temperature for thirty minutes. This will give excellent results of fine detail and the glass will fill in the depressions thicker than the raised areas, but not thin so much in raised areas as to become fragile. Three layers of glass will form an architecturally sound tile that could be cemented in place.

Annealing times should be two to three times longer than for the same thickness of glass without the mold material. Follow the basic rule: anneal for the thickest part of the glass plus the thickness of the mold material. Annealing graph in the technical information section of this book can guide you as to time and temperatures for specific thicknesses.

Carving castables for bas-relief is an inexpensive process that can add great dimension to your fused work. Plaster relief molds are technically easy to understand and pose no health hazards, other than airborn plaster dust or silica. Wear a dust mask when appropriate.

CHAPTER TWO

Glory Hole

A glory hole is an insulated container with an open front and a heat source capable of producing intense heat. The glory hole is used for quick and localized heating and reheating of glass, usually held on the end of a punty rod. Use of a glory hole allows a glass fuser to make stringer, pattern bars, fracture glass (confetti), or free form trailed lines as design elements to be used in fused glass work.

Glory hole made from a small octagon kiln turned on its side.

Boyce tests Doug Pomeroy's homemade glory hole, consisting of a fiber lined six-gallon bucket and pipe fittings. In this test the glory hole ran for eight hours on five gallons of propane.

Doug's glory hole and burner and his commercial griddle marver.

Opposite page: Design bars by Jennifer Larkin Haskins.
"Face Bowl #5", 5-1/2" in diameter, Jennifer Larkin Haskins.

Cross sections of design bars made by heating and stretching pre-fired bundles, with a glory hole as the heat source.

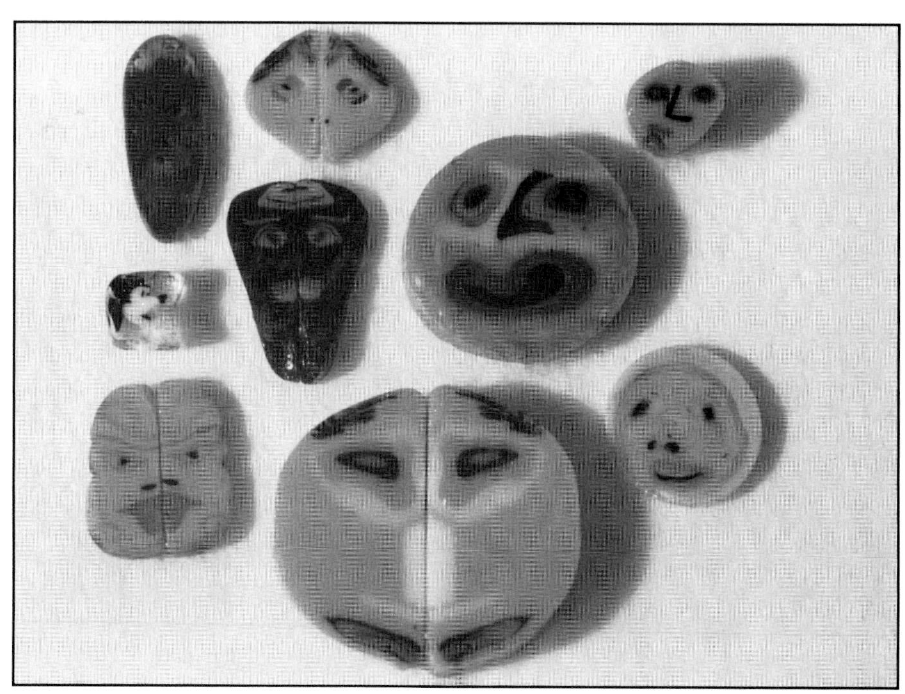

Cut sections of face designs, where the completed motif is created by opposing cross sections from pattern bars that are made to provide only half of the design.

Slicing pattern bars with a chop saw with diamond blade, a singularly important piece of equipment for the studio where slices of pattern bars will be used in design.

Design Bundles which were overfired and slumped onto their sides, can be picked up and straightened in the glory hole.

Pattern bars that have been laminated together by firing in a fusing kiln can be formed and stretched using a glory hole. The stacks of glass that become the pick-ups or "gathers" on the end of the punty should be fused together enough to form one piece, but it is not necessary to have them fully fused. Bullseye glass laminates at 1350°F without deforming a great deal, leaving the design crisp. Bundles can be made by twisting copper wire around the group of stacked pieces (chosen and placed so as to create a design), which are then stood on end for laminating in a top loading kiln, or made by laying bundles on their sides in a front loading kiln.

The bundles can be placed on one side of the kiln shelf, leaving the other side free to hold the finished objects for annealing. The kiln is fired to 1350°F, held there until the glass has laminated, then lowered to 1100°F before pieces are picked up on the punty. *Always turn off the kiln before putting the metal rod into it to pick up glass.*

The glory hole segment of the forming is begun by preparing a punty rod to pick up a large bundle of glass. The punty rod tip is heated to red heat in the glory hole and then touched to a small piece (approximately 1 1/2" X 1 1/2") of preheated glass in the fusing kiln and withdrawn from the kiln. This glass is then heated in the glory hole until it forms a small ball on the end of the punty. It is marvered (rolled on a steel plate) to shape it and cool it slightly on the outside. The punty is then used to pick up the bundle of glass from the fusing kiln, using the small wad to stick the bundle to the punty. The bundle is heated in the glory hole until it reaches working temperature

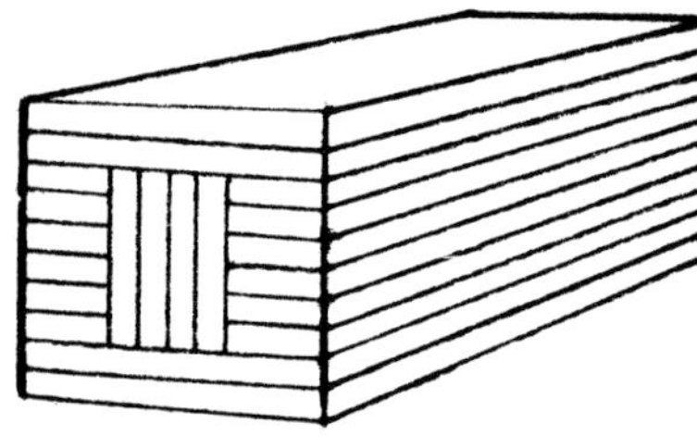

Bundles of glass may be laid up flat or vertical and wired together.

(1600°F to 1800°F). It is periodically removed from the glory hole during the heating process to form it on the marver. A square bundle can be rolled round or shaped with carbon paddles to maintain its squareness or to take the shape of a triangle. The bundle is worked slowly, reheating and forming, shaping with paddles, then reheating again, in order to maintain control.

The bundle, when handled properly, will get longer as the air is squeezed out from between the layers of glass. When the design bundle has been fully fused in the glory hole, it should be uniform in temperature and hot enough to stretch when pulled with a pair of shears or when swung upside down with a pendulum action. When the pattern bar is the desired shape and length, a file that has been dipped in water is used to score the glass very close to the end of the punty, where it is attached to the glass. The finished bar is placed back in the hot kiln by setting it on the kiln shelf and striking the punty with a sharp blow in approximately the center of the rod. This will create a shock wave that travels down the punty rod, causing the hot bar to crack off the punty at the score made by the file.

Pattern bars that start with a stack of glass 1 1/2" X 1 1/2" X 5" may be formed into a 3/4" square approximately 12" long. The design will remain the same as that originally stacked into the glass, but be proportionally smaller. If the pattern bar is stretched too far the pattern will remain but be hard to discern.

Small cane and twists can be cut into shorter lengths with tile nipping pliers.

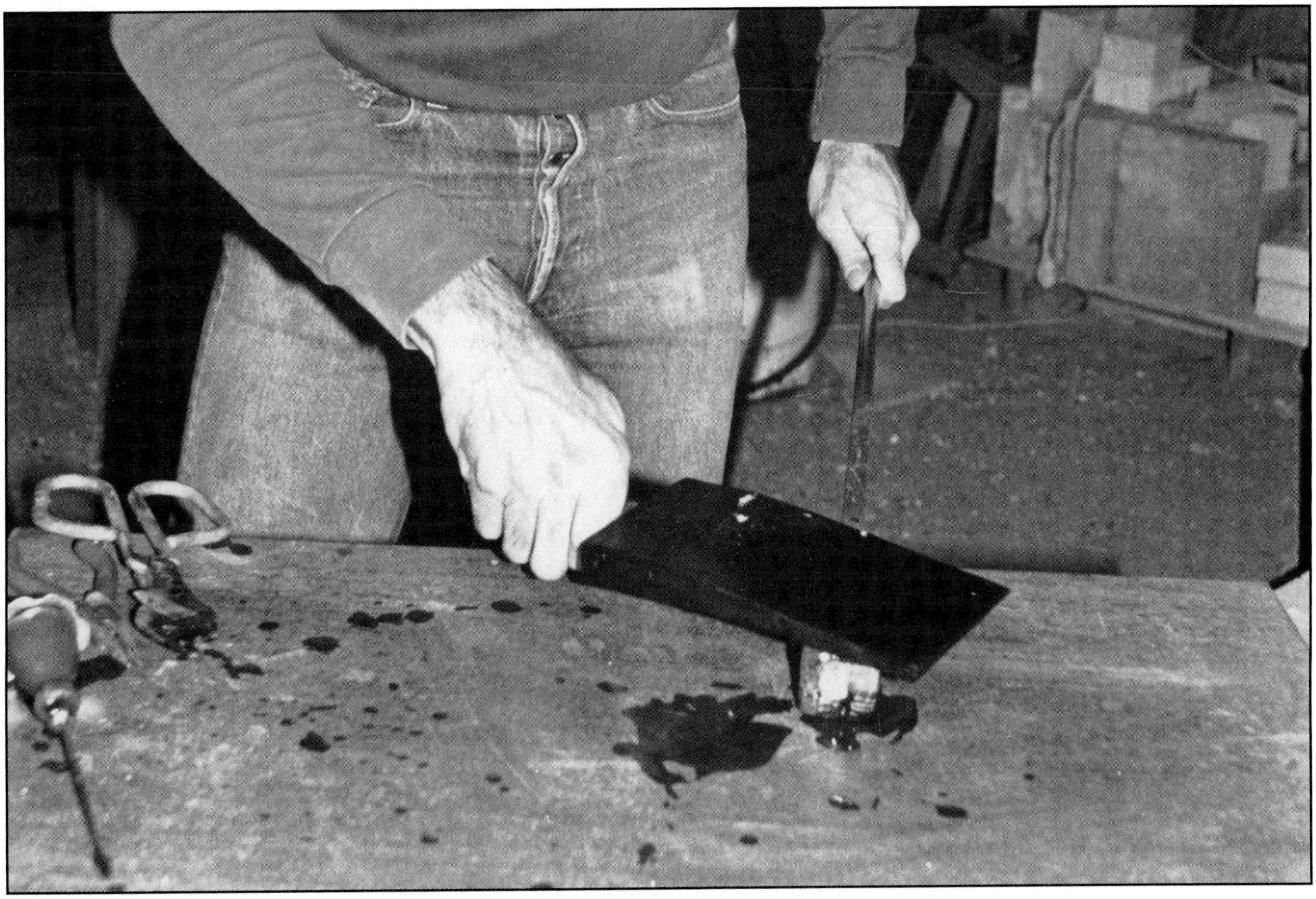

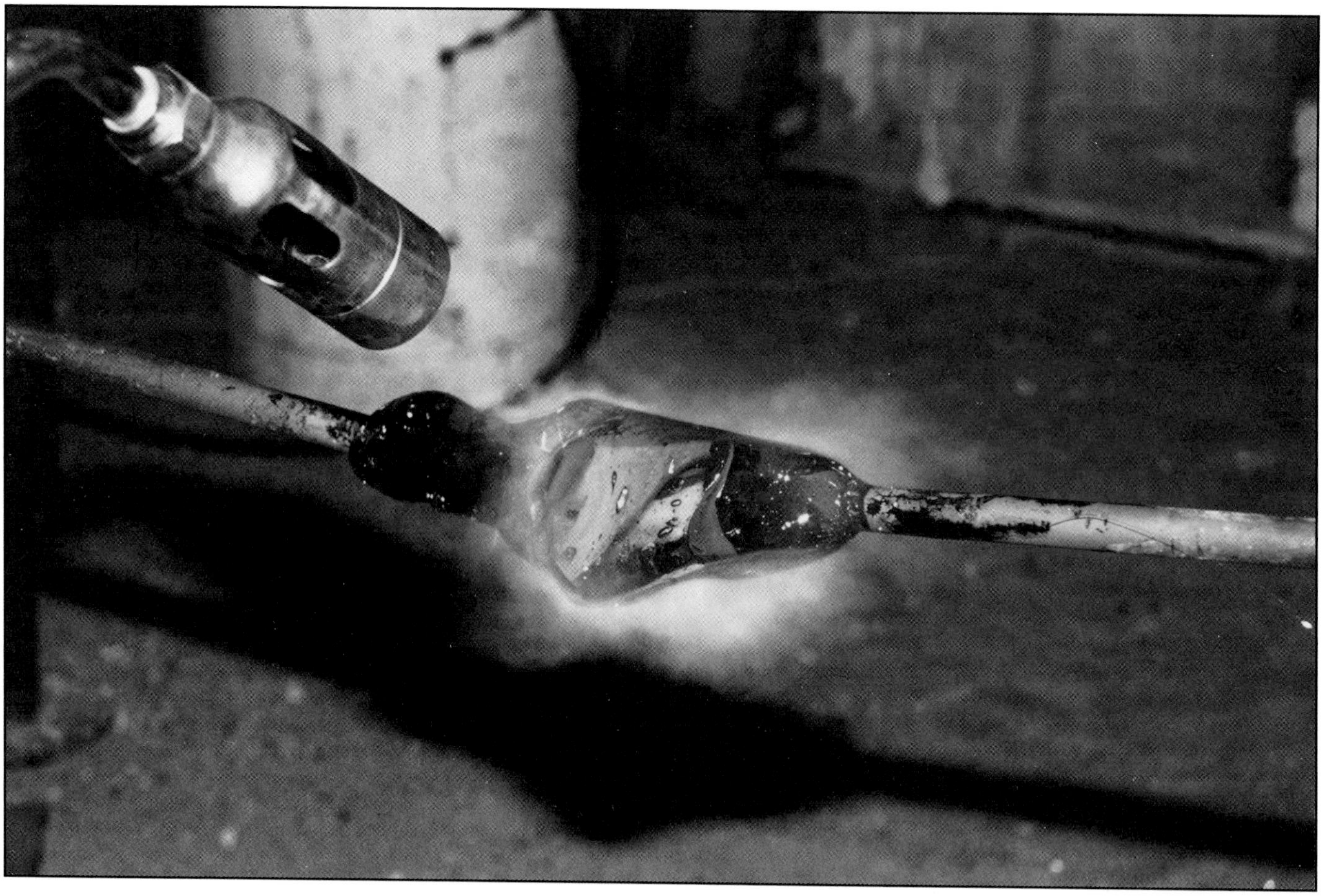

Applying heat to a specific area of a bundle, the thickest part, with a hand-held propane torch. This will assist in getting more finished cane with a common sized section.

Diamond shears are used to pull, cut or crimp glass.

The process of using a glory hole to make pattern bars applies to making other shapes and designs. In making stringer glass or 1/4" rod, a solid colored bundle is picked up from the fusing oven, heated in the glory hole, shaped on the marver (usually round), and then one end is hooked in a V groove in a standing board or around a nail in the workbench. The glassworker walks backwards, holding the punty at bench height, drawing out the glass into a small thread (stringer). If he walks slowly and not as far, a rod is made. If the glass on the punty is flattened before stretching, a ribbon of glass is made.

Glass formed by this method does not have to be annealed if its largest cross section is 3/16" or smaller. Larger sections should be placed back in the fusing kiln for annealing.

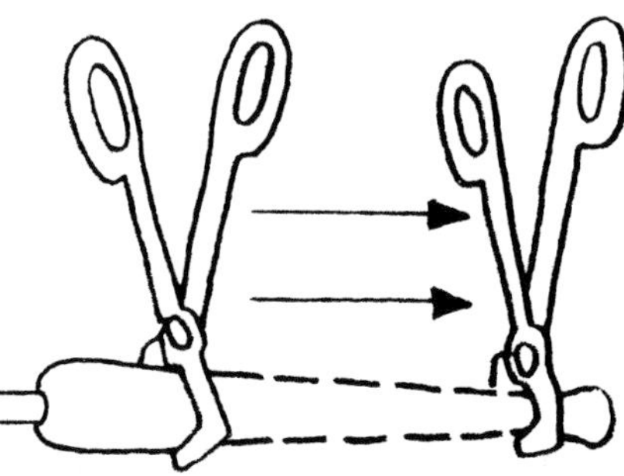

Peter and Joan working together to make twisted rod.

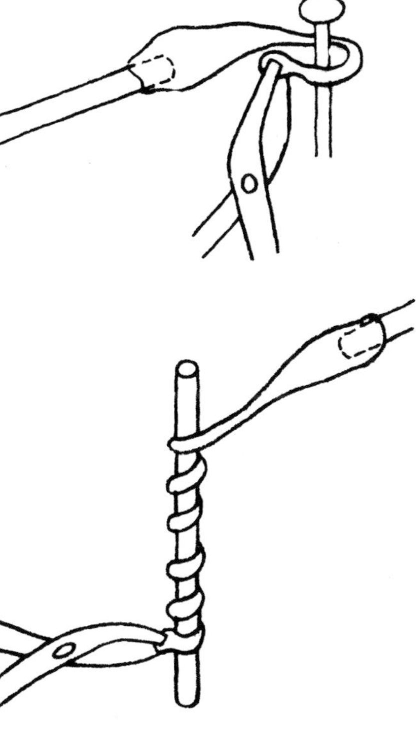

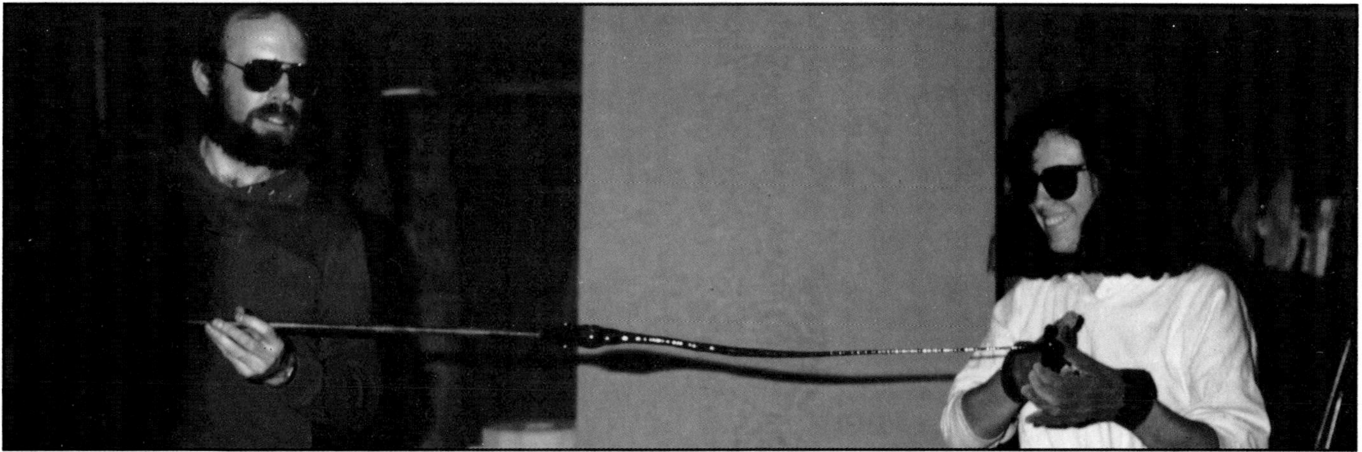

GLASS BLOWING

With a glory hole added to a fusing studio the result is close to meeting the needs of a hot glass shop. The glass can be worked in its most molten state with this simple piece of equipment. The experience of stretching glass stringer or pattern bar leads most people to think of picking up bundles on a hollow pipe (blow pipe) and blowing a bubble. And why not?

I think there are some reasons: the amount of glass you can pick up out of your fusing kiln is very limited. You can experience a bubble, but you can't do much with it. In addition, it is very difficult and time consuming to form the glass into the proper gather for blowing when your equipment consists of a kiln and a glory hole. There are much better ways to learn glass blowing. And what you learn, starting with bundles in a fusing studio with a glory hole, may have to be unlearned when you have the opportunity to make gathers of molten glass from a glass furnace. If you want to blow glass, build a small crucible furnace and do it right.

CONFETTI

If you want to make thin glass fractures or "confetti" by blowing out bundles, "fusing oven blowing" will work. Fractures are the very thin pieces of glass sometimes fused to the back side of sheets of glass, creating a confetti effect, as in Bullseye or Uroborus fracture-streamer glass. This glass is made by gathering glass when it is very hot and injecting enough air into the gather quickly enough to stretch the bubble out to the thinness of paper.

Dan Schuster, at Bullseye Glass Company, blowing large bubbles for fractures to be used in sheet glass. Glass blowing on this scale requires a pot furnace, glory hole, and compressed air.

After the glass bubble is air cooled it is broken and the small chips can be fused into other glass. Fractures will roll up and change shape if they are fused on the surface of glass, but will keep their shape if placed on the fusing shelf and covered with sheet glass.

Free form trailings or streamers can also be made with bundles picked up from a fusing kiln, but are more easily made by gathering from a crucible. The glass bundle must be super-heated in the glory hole, turning the punty rapidly between thumb and index finger in order to keep the glass from dripping off the punty rod. Just before the glass drips off the rod, it is withdrawn from the glory hole and whipped back and forth over a non-combustible floor (concrete is fine). The resulting free form lines look a lot like vines or other natural lines. In a variation of this process, the lines are made larger and more controlled, forming them on a hot marving table, then moving them to the annealing oven on a flat wood paddle. This process is discussed in more detail in the discussion of crucible melting in this book.

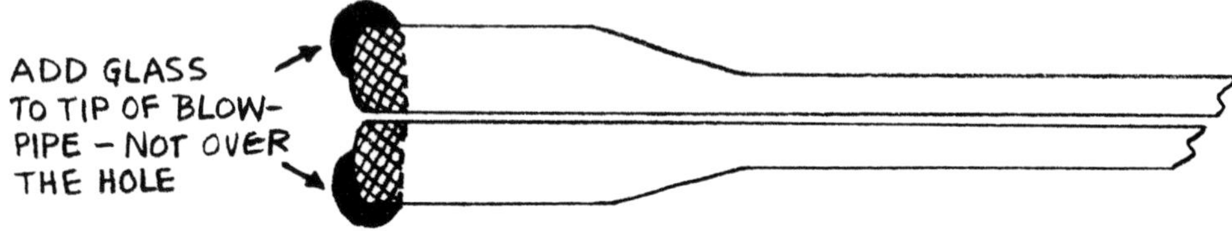

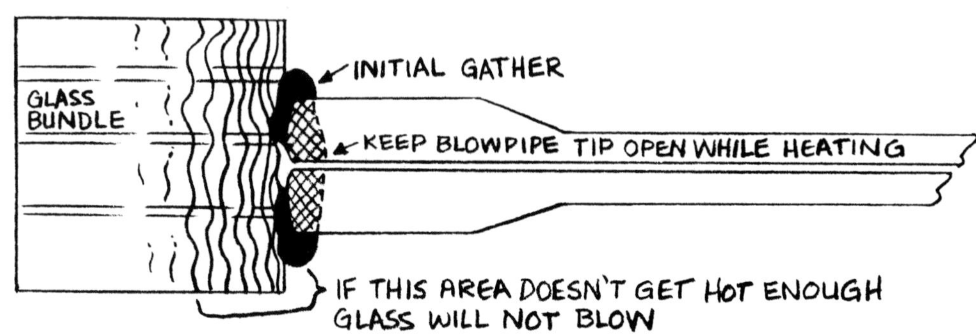

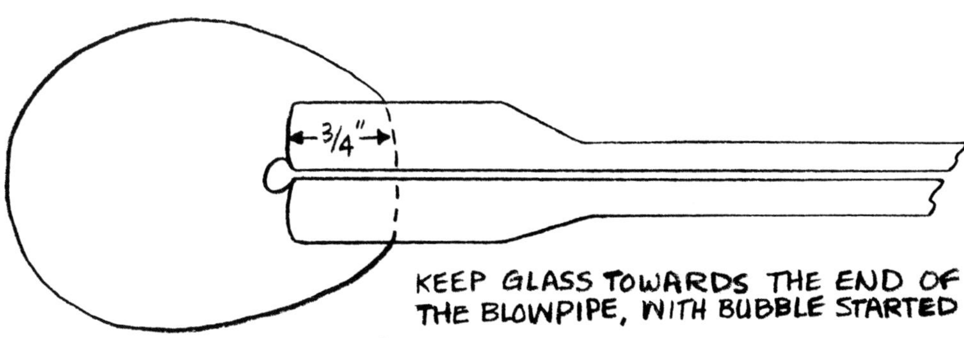

TOOLS

The basic tools needed for hot glass working can be purchased from glass blowing equipment companies (listed in the suppliers section) or made at home. All the equipment can be built by the enterprising glass worker who can find a kind soul in a welding shop.

Punties, gathering irons and blow pipes are usually made from stainless steel. A piece of stainless rod 50" to 54" long, 1/2" in diameter, with a stop collar and a piece of rubber hose for a handle makes an excellent punty rod. A section of cold rolled steel with a 6" X 1/2" stainless tip welded on the end is a lot cheaper and works as well. Blow pipes usually have machined tips of stainless bar stock welded to light weight stainless pipe. They can be very expensive and are not necessary to the beginning or weekend glass blower.

To make a blow pipe, purchase a five foot length of 1/2" black pipe. Arc weld five to ten stainless beads around one end to build up a bell shaped collar (see graphic). Be sure to continue the stainless weld around the end of the pipe, slightly closing off the 1/2" opening. Drill out the end to 3/8". The stainless steel covers the portion of the steel pipe that will be dipped into the glass, thereby keeping the steel slag from spalling into the glass.

HOMEMADE BLOWPIPE

MOUTHPIECE
GARDEN HOSE HANDLE
1/2" BLACK IRON PIPE
STAINLESS, WELDED & GROUND

LARGE END PUNTIE

1/2" GATHERING END

PUNTIE, 6" STAINLESS TIP

SHOVEL, FOR CHARGING FURNACE

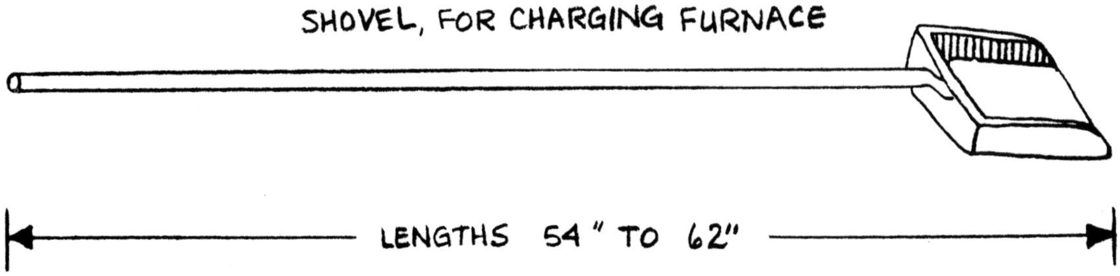

LENGTHS 54" TO 62"

9½" TRIMMING SHEARS

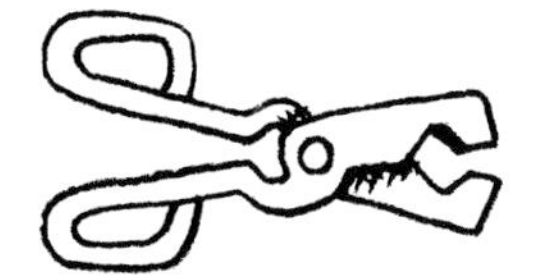

10" DIAMOND SHEARS

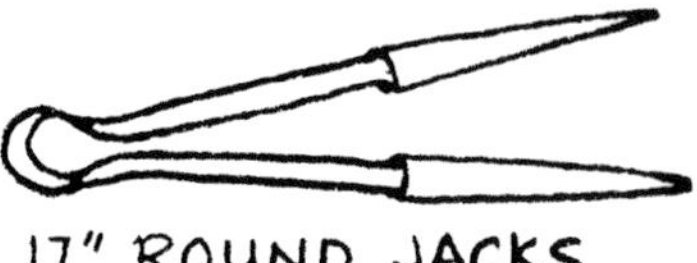

17" ROUND JACKS

12" TWEEZERS

FRUIT WOOD BLOCKS

The stainless weld can be ground until smooth on any home grinder, then sanded with #80 carbide sandpaper. A mouthpiece is made from a male air hose coupling modified on a grinder. Sand the pipe with #80 sandpaper and oil it with any kind of oil between uses. It is advisable to make more than one pipe at a time, since most of the expense is running down all the parts and locating a sympathetic welder.

Trimming shears and diamond shears are used for cutting the glass while it is hot. Tin snips work well as glass shears. Grind the side opposite the cutting surface to make snips thinner. This will make your glass cut easier because you don't have to displace so much uncut glass with the thick steel. Japanese garden scissors work well if the handles are extended.

To make diamond shears, grind two V cuts in a pair of lawn shears and sharpen the V cut on the outside surface only (see graphic). I started with home made shears, but if I were to buy one tool, it would be a pair of small diamond shears from a company like Steinert.

Fruit wood paddles can be used for forming the glass. Any green wood works well enough, but fruit woods are best, having less pitch than many other woods. Cut the forming paddles out on a bandsaw, making them flat and comfortable to the hand. Keep all your wood tools in water and dip them in water after each time they are in contact with the hot glass. The idea is to char the wood evenly across the work area, forming a carbon layer that doesn't burn because the wood is wet.

The marving plate, or marver, is any flat surface used to roll and shape the glass against when it is on the punty or blow pipe. Cast iron commercial griddle stove tops work well. Half inch steel plate or pieces of polished castings can be found at scrap yards. The thickness and size of the marver you need is dependent on the amount of glass and the kind of work you plan to do. If you are marvering small pickups from the fusing kiln, 1/4" plate steel one foot by two feet will work great. But if you plan on pouring crucibles of molten glass, four pounds at a time, on its surface, drawing thick trailed lines, or rolling small sheets of glass, a larger and thicker piece of steel is necessary.

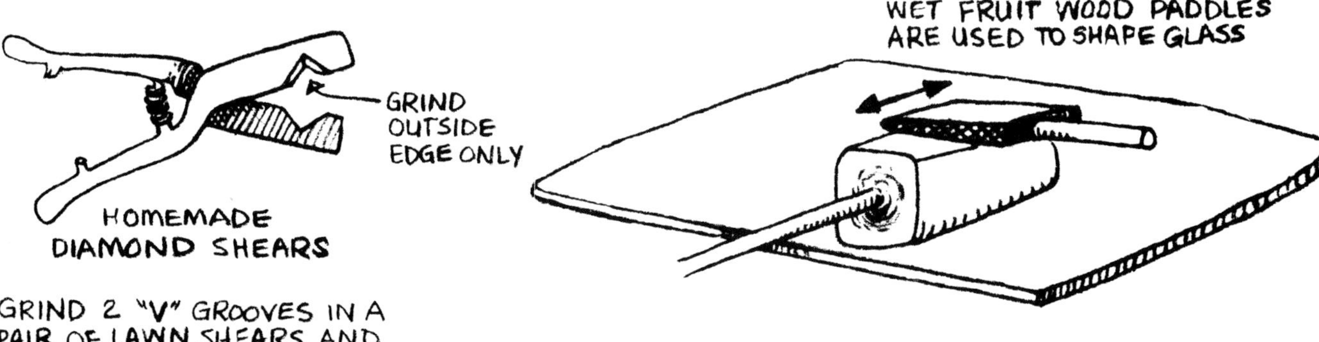

GRIND 2 "V" GROOVES IN A PAIR OF LAWN SHEARS AND SHARPEN "V" CUT ON OUTSIDE SURFACE ONLY

BUILDING A GLORY HOLE

A glory hole is an insulated drum or other container that is used for reheating glass during various stages of forming. It does not contain any glass and should be able to maintain a temperature of 150°F hotter than the gathering temperature of the glass being worked (approximately 2000°F). A glory hole for glass working often takes the form of a bucket turned on its side and fired with a gas burner. The burner should be sized to heat the insulated container to 2000°F, or past the working temperature of the glass that is being worked.

Some glory holes are built so that the heat comes specifically from the flame and others use predominantly reflected heat from the walls of the glory hole. The glory hole is turned on just before work starts and should heat up in ten minutes. It is turned off when work is done and will cool quickly, if built from fiber blanket insulation. The best safety insurance is to always be present when the glory hole is on or cooling.

There are presently two glory holes on the market. One is the Murphy Fire Bucket, made by Fusion Glass, Inc.; the other is made by Denver Machinery. Most glory holes are home made and are seen in many "off hand" glass blower's studios. The following descriptions and pictures of building a glory hole comprise a report of how I have built glory holes in my studio.

A table-top glory hole used in our studio. A materials list and construction diagram are provided on the following pages.

Another glory hole, designed by Rob Doglass Ross. It is a combination glory hole/annealer, with a damper between the two chambers to allow exhaust heat from the glory hole to be used by the annealer.

BUILDING YOUR OWN GLORY HOLE

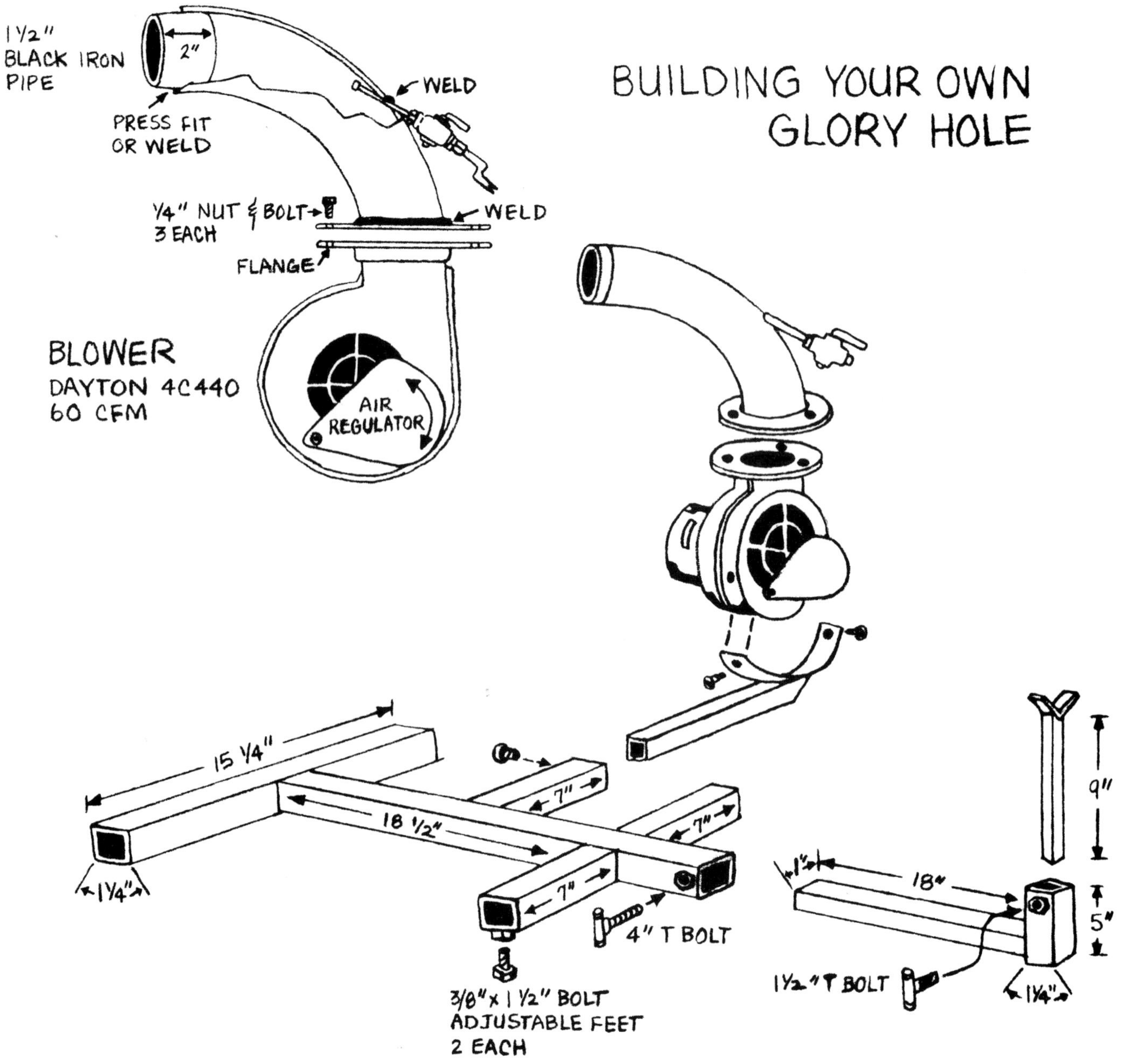

1½" BLACK IRON PIPE
2"
PRESS FIT OR WELD
WELD
¼" NUT & BOLT 3 EACH
WELD
FLANGE
BLOWER
DAYTON 4C440
60 CFM
AIR REGULATOR
15 ¼"
18 ½"
7"
7"
7"
1¼"
4" T BOLT
3/8" x 1 ½" BOLT
ADJUSTABLE FEET
2 EACH
9"
1"
18"
5"
1½" T BOLT
1¼"

BURNER TIP ASSEMBLY

1/8" BLACK IRON PIPE
1/16" HOLE
4"
1/8" CAP
REDUCER
GAS VALVE
GAS LINE TO REGULATOR

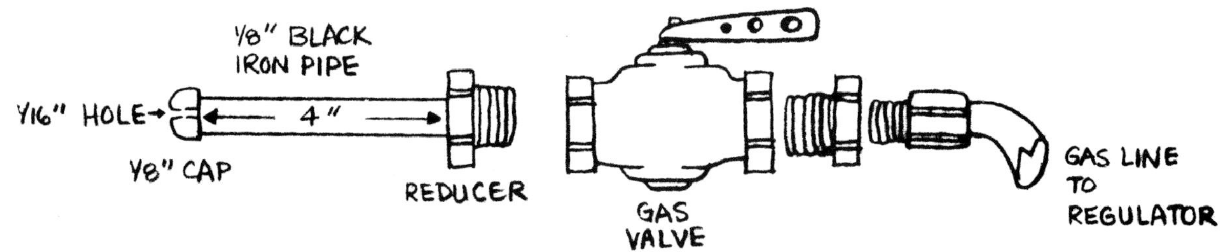

MATERIALS

1. Metal container or rolled steel drum with lid (17" x 20" approx).
2. One roll of fiber blanket (6 # density, 2' x 25', 50 sq. ft).
3. One gallon of refractory cement (such as Sairset or A.P. Green #36).
4. One Dayton blower #4C440.
5. 1 1/4" sq. steel tubing, 6 ft. long, 16-14 gauge.
6. 1" sq. steel tubing, 4 ft long.
7. 1" x 1/8" flat steel bar for blower mount, 12" long.
8. 5 - 3/8" nuts.
9. 4 - 3/8" x 1 1/4" bolts
10. 1- 3/8"x4" bolt
11. One right angle exhaust pipe with flange.
12. Cord and plug for blower.
13. 5 ft. Nichrome wire, 16-20 guage.
14. 2 inches of 1 1/2" diameter black pipe (no threads).

The initial concept for this glory hole was to design one that could be built in any city. All the materials except the fiber blanket can be purchased in most large hardware stores. Fiber blanket can be purchased from many companies listed in the suppliers section of this book. Normal shop tools plus a metal cutting blade for a power jig saw are all that is needed.

BUILDING PROCEDURES

1. Build stand and blower mount by welding assorted lengths of 1 1/4" square tubing together.
2. Weld back on steel drum.
3. Weld blower mount and punty rest.
4. Cut hole for burner port with hacksaw.
5. Line the steel drum with fiber blanket, after welding drum to stand. Cut sizes of fiber blanket for 17" x 20" steel drum, i.e. first layer 50 1/2" x 17 1/2", second layer 48" x 17 1/2", third layer 37 1/2" x 17 1/2".
6. Add two 12" circles to finish back of glory hole.
7. Cut three 17" circles of fiber blanket with 6" hole in the center for door pieces; wire to metal door with nichrome wire.
8. Cover all exposed fiber surfaces with refractory cement that has been thinned with water by 50%. Let dry, then add a second coat (Add 30 mesh silica sand to water and refractory cement for second coat).
9. Complete burner by bolting together, adding electrical cord, exhaust tubing and burner tip.
10. Add gas pressure regulator, hose and gas shut- off valve (this can often be purchased as one unit referred to as a gas weed burner).

OPERATING AND SAFETY

Setting up the studio arrangement, especially the location of kiln in relation to glory hole, should be well thought out in advance of beginning any glory hole work. The fusing kiln should be close enough to the glory hole work area that the glass doesn't crack or fracture from cooling too much on the way between the two heat sources. Once you learn the steps, as much as fifteen feet is reasonable. Have another glass worker there to help you; it takes two people until you have mastered all the moves. Once you have learned and are confident, it is possible to work alone.

Lighting a glory hole for the first time can be a hair raising experience. It is very easy to be timid, but if you follow good safety procedures, you should avoid problems.

1. Always keep the propane tank six to ten feet behind the glory hole. Keep the path to the tank clear. You can shut off the gas at the tank.
2. Always have a gas turn-off handle close to the burner and separate from the main on/off valve on the tank.
3. Operate the burner from the burner, not from the tank.
4. Turn on the air blower and cover 1/2 of the air intake. This cuts down the volume of the air.
5. Turn the gas on at the tank, but not at the burner.
6. Light a small hand-held propane torch to light the burner, not a match. Hold the flame in front of the burner port, but not so close that the moving air blows out the flame.
7. Turn on the gas at the burner *one half.* The burner should light right away, unless the gas line is full of air. As long as the flame on the hand-held torch is on, you are not at risk.
8. Adjust the gas so that a small flame (wispy blue-yellow) can be seen burning outside the hole in the front. After the glory hole is red hot on the surface of the fiber (about two minutes), adjust for more air, by opening the flap on the blower.

9. It is possible to achieve oxidation or reduction with a gas burner. Each of these conditions will heat the chamber differently and will affect your glass differently. Practical knowledge about glory hole atmosphere and temperature, gained by practice with the procedures, will be most helpful.
10. When turning off the glory hole, *always turn off the gas first, leaving the air blower on for five minutes.*

It is always advisable to have a pair of high temperature heat resistant gloves close by when working with a glory hole, but do not wear gloves while working the glass on a punty or a blowpipe. If the punty is too hot, cool it with water by splashing on it or by running a small hose to the work area for applying cool water. The rod or pipe can be cooled with water while a glass piece is on the end, up to six inches from the glass piece, without thermal shocking the glass.

Do not leave a glory hole running unattended, unless you have added safety shutoff valves and have the glory hole under a metal hood. Always wear safety glasses while using a glory hole.

CHAPTER THREE

Stringer

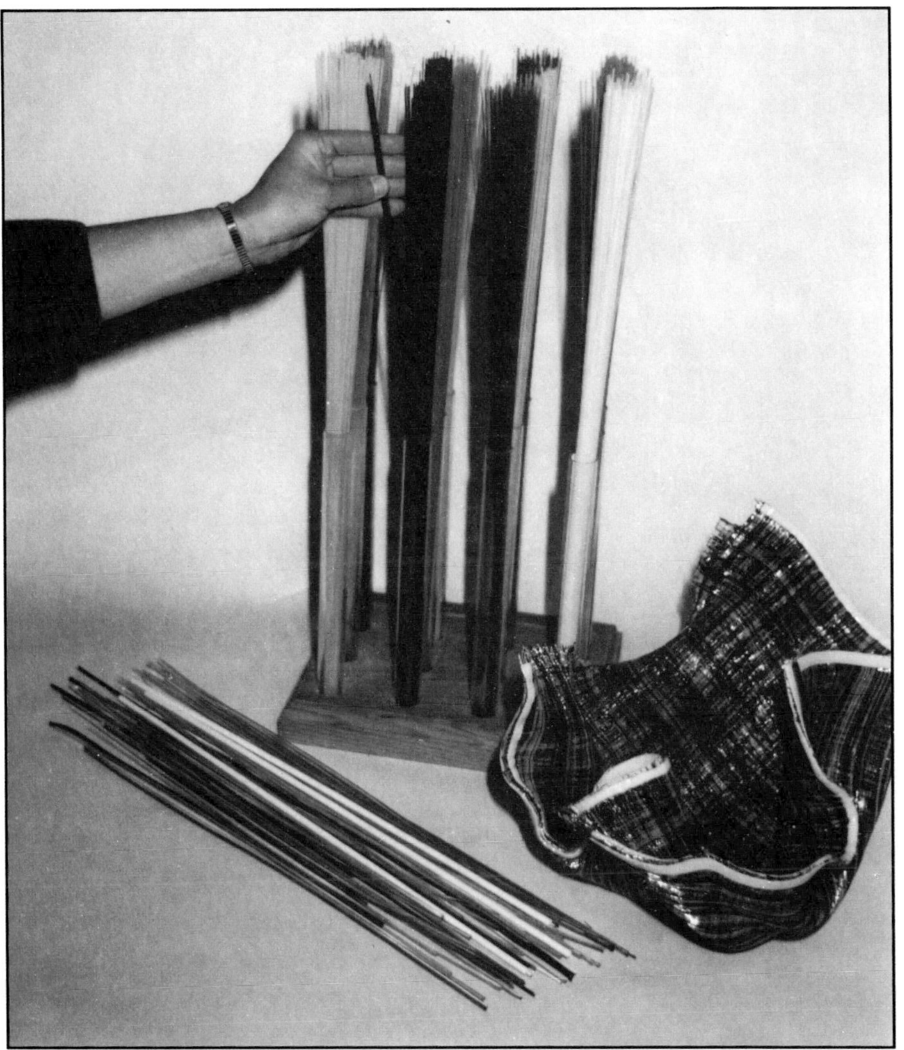

This mask uses glass stringer for detail lines.

An array of two-foot lengths of glass stringer (in display stand), glass rod (in foreground), and a fused stringer bowl.

Glass stringers are thinly drawn filaments of glass the diameter of pencil lead or common household string. When small quantities are needed, stringer can be made in the studio. Narrow strips are cut from sheets of glass, heated in the flame of a torch until the glass begins to ball up, then stretched between two pairs of pliers as far as the reach of the arms will permit. The thin cross section of the glass is small enough that it will anneal in the air without insulation.

Larger quantities of stringer are made by gathering glass from a crucible, attaching one end of the molten gather to a nail on a bench, then walking away from the bench while holding the punty rod at the height of the bench. Even larger quantities can be made by top draw or bottom draw glass crucible machinery. Several glass distributors in the United States offer glass stringer in an array of colors ready to use in fused glass designs.

Glass stringer more than one-eighth inch in diameter is referred to as glass rod. This is made by the same techniques described above, pulling the molten glass more slowly to get results with a larger diameter.

Opposite page: Stringer bowl, Linda Ellis Andrews.
A group of large stringer bowls by Dan Ott.

Closeup of stringer "fabric".

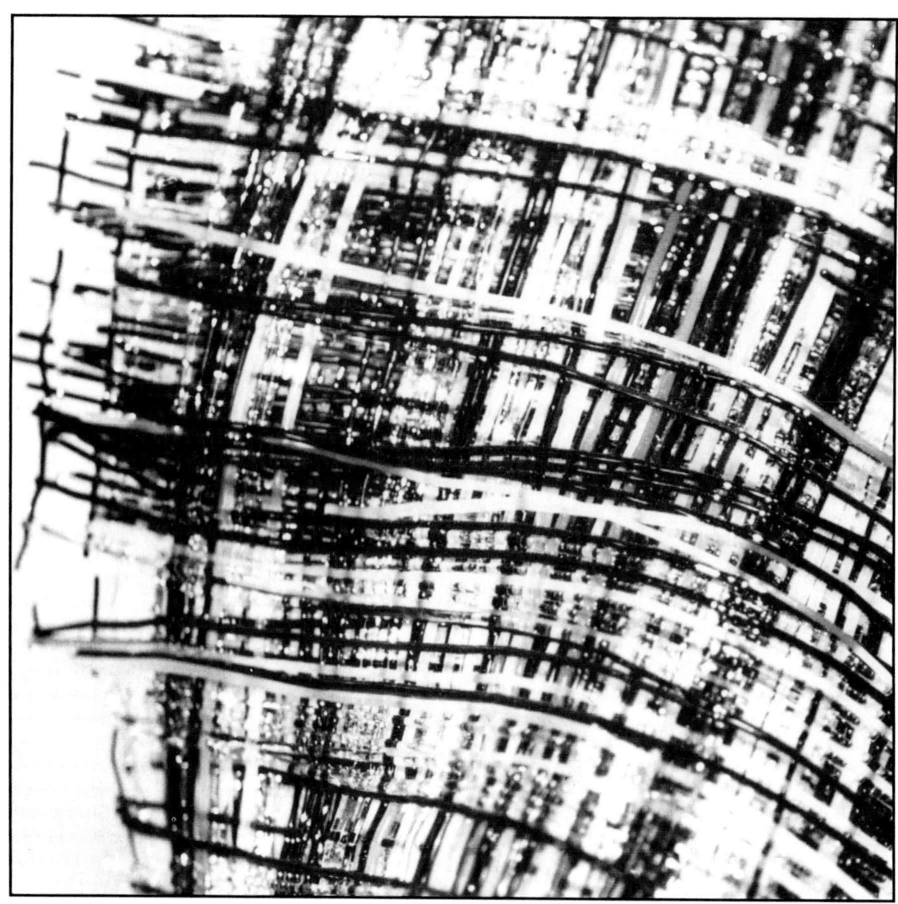

Freeform stringer napkin bowl, using stringer and glass rod.

Streamers are free-form stringer made by gathering glass from a crucible or open hearth furnace on a punty rod and, while the glass is still very runny, whipping the punty back and forth, allowing the glass to stream onto a marvering plate or concrete floor. These free-form glass threads are generally referred to as streamers.

Both straight stringer and curved free-form streamers allow designers of fused glass work to easily achieve line detail in their work. When used in massive quantities they can be fused to themselves, without other glass, so that a sort of "fabric" is the result They can be fused onto a blank of sheet glass for strong textural effects. Straight stringer stacks well, so a patient craftsman can stack stringer into design bundles, fuse the bundles, and slice cross sections that look much like a pointalist drawing.

Dan Ott removes fused stringer "fabric" from the hot kiln (1400°F) and folds it into a stainless steel bowl. The mold and the stringer form are then placed back in the kiln for annealing.

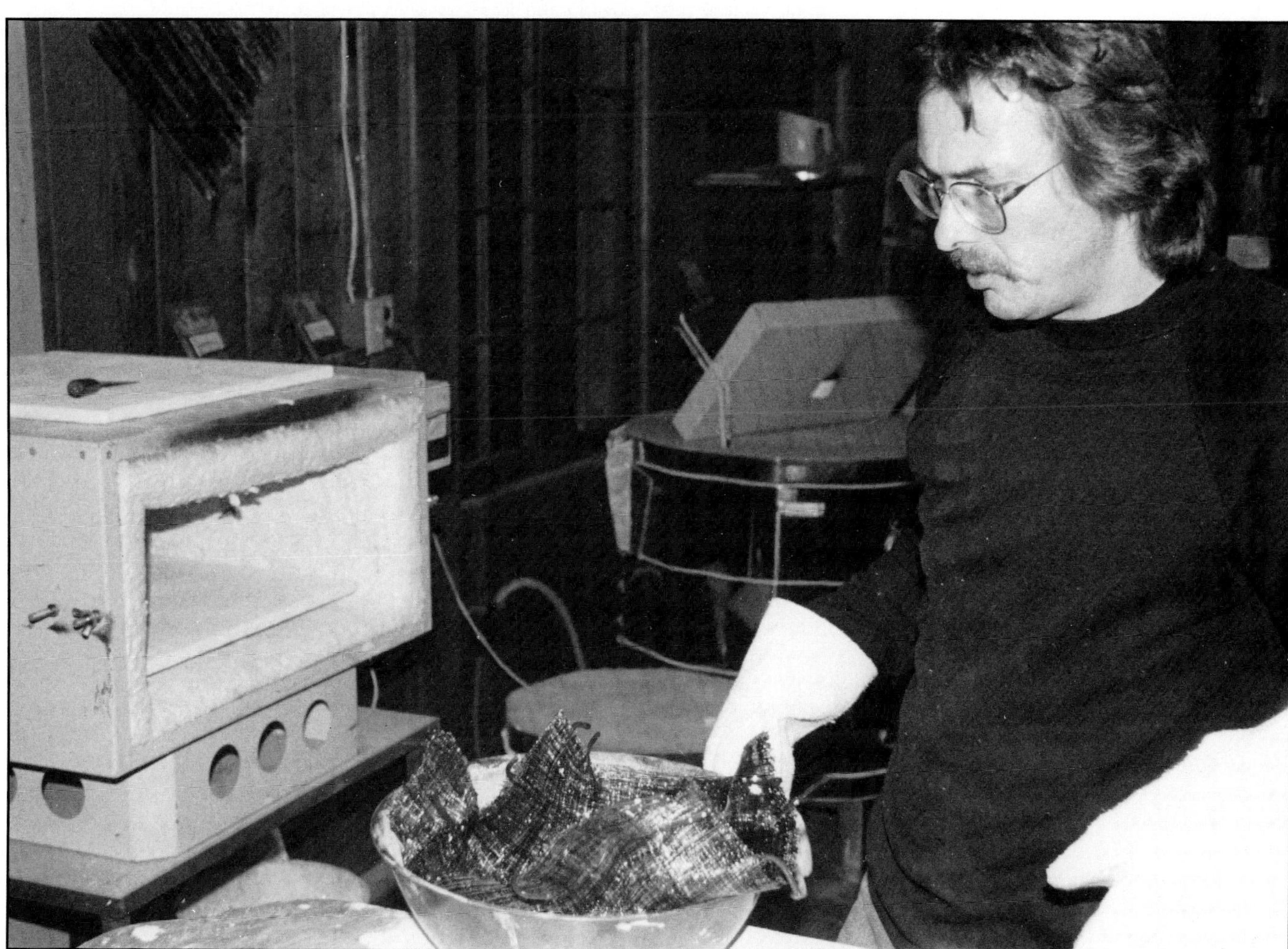

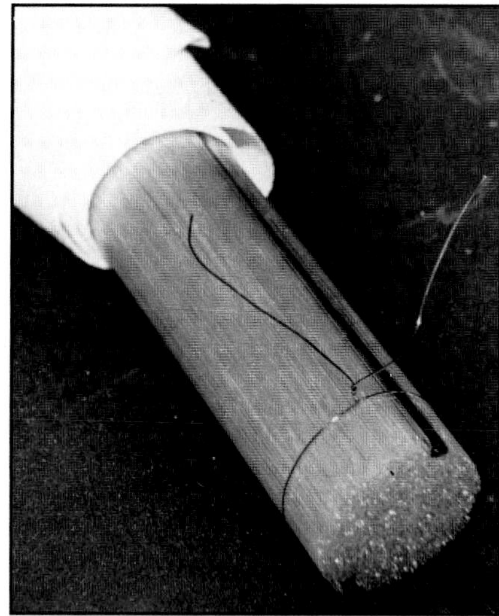

A bundle of stringer, laid up to achieve a chosen design in cross section, wrapped in fiber paper, tied with wire. Stood on end for fusing, the resulting design can be used by cutting sections with a diamond band saw, or reworked as cane in a glory hole.

Stringer laid up for fusing.

Dan shaping fused stringer sheet over a stainless steel bowl, which must be removed before annealing.

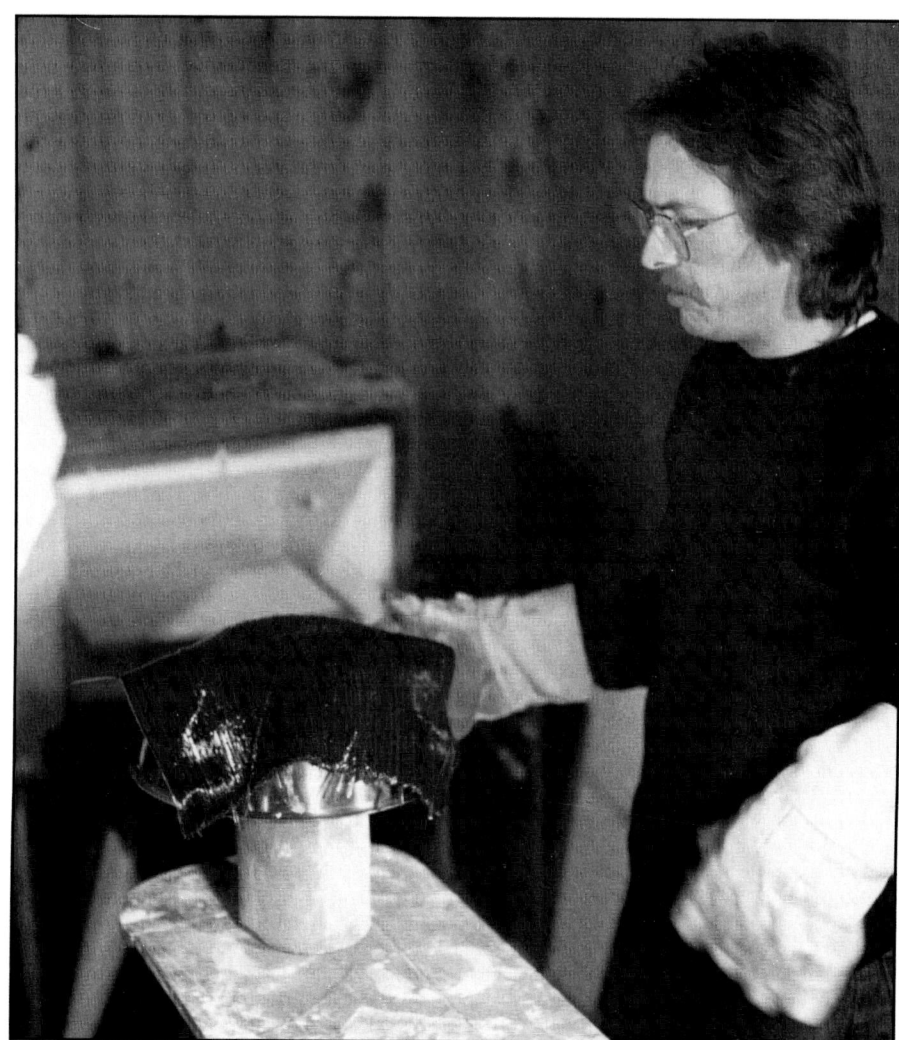

Stringer can be re-worked in a low torch flame or candle flame to create curved lines. It can be barely melted and attached to itself so that line drawings with great detail are the result, but this technique requires practice. A good way to handle the glass in this manner is to work it on a cast iron or steel plate that is kept hot on an electric hot plate. The stringer section is held in one hand and a propane hand torch in the other. Heating the glass stringer just before it touches the metal plate and pushing it into the plate in a continuous curved line allows the effect of a controlled line drawing. When the plate cools, the drawing will release. I have observed many individual techniques that represent a subtle variation of this style of glass drawing. This very simiplified explanation gives you a good idea of how to get started, but the subtleties of control in handling the glass will come with patience and perseverance.

The bold use of glass stringer for design is one of the more recent innovations that has occurred since the reintroduction of glass fusing. This is a result of the persistent search for new ways of seeing kiln fired glass, as well as the general availability, in recent years, of well-made, affordable glass stringer. The possibilities for fine detail, pre-formed lines, glass pointilist drawings, and entire weavings of glass fabric are being used by a few glass artists, but the potential of the product, used by itself or in conjunction with sheet glass, has not been fully explored.

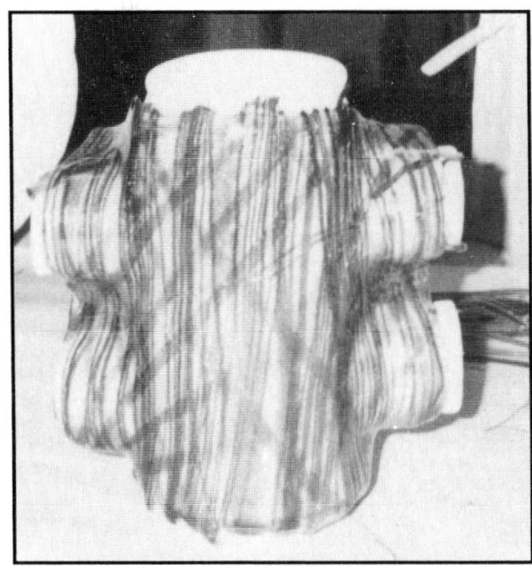

Glass stringer and rod fused and slumped over a bisque stoneware vase. The vase may be removed and used to slump another sheet of glass over its opposite side, so that the two slumped sheets will meet to form a drapery, which is glued where the sheets meet. The clay form remains as part of the finished piece.

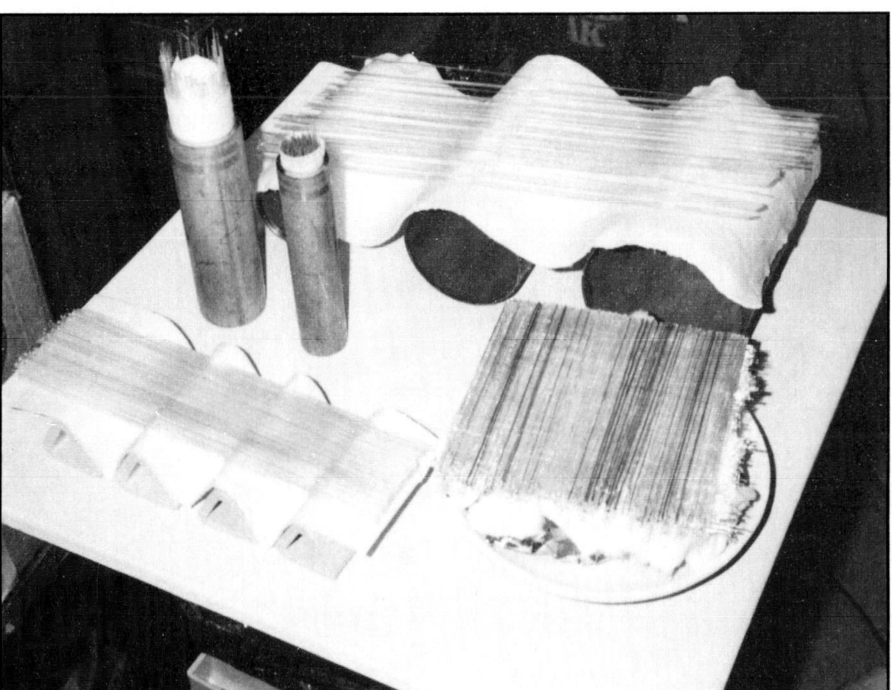

Stringer may be slumped as individual pieces to create curves for design elements in fused artwork.

Making streamers. The glass is heated to near-liquid state in a glory hole, and let drip from the punty rod while it is whipped back and forth over a non-flammable surface.

Freeform streamers may be used as design elements. Here they are arranged, contained by a fiber dam, and are being covered with frit.

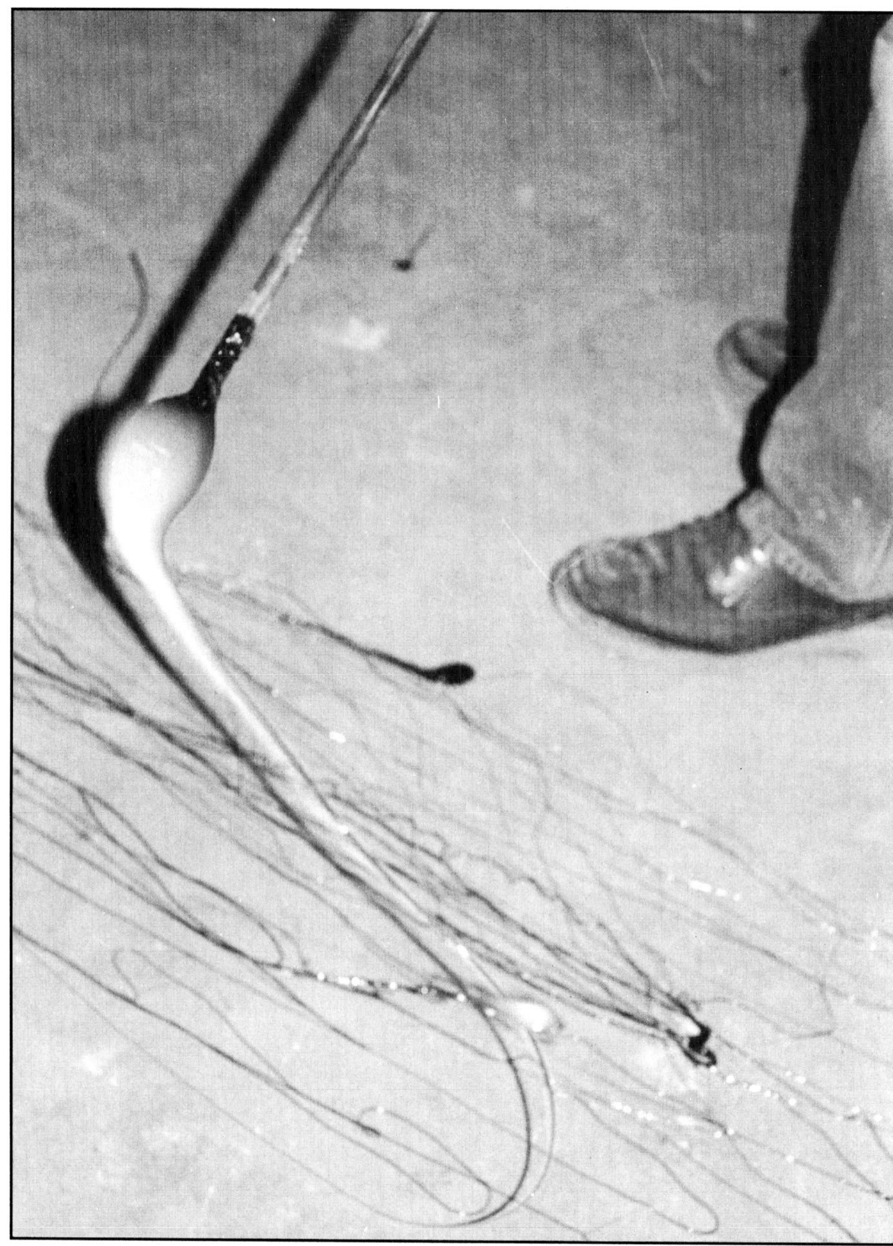

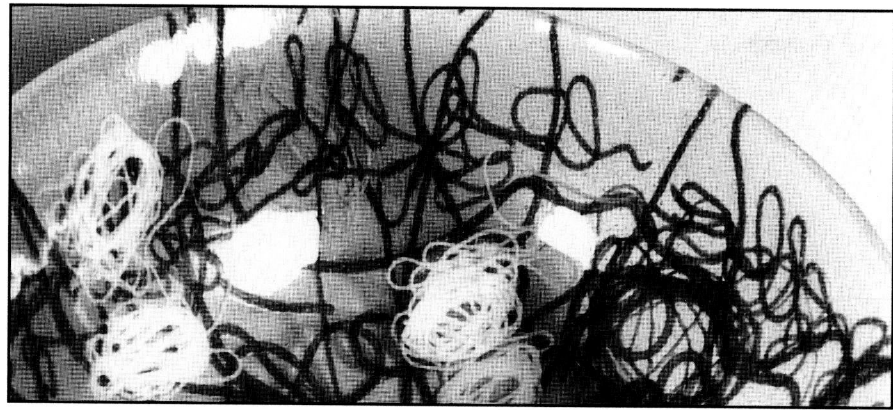

Sculptural bowl, by Boyce Lundstrom. Stringer "fabric" fused to an arrangement of pre-fused black triangles; bowl shape achieved by hand manipulation, during fusing.

One-inch thick glass tile, by Boyce Lundstrom, made of clear cullet and an array of colored freeform streamers. The base is stoneware.

Fan vase, by Linda Ellis Andrews, glass slumped over a clay vase, then glued to the vase, used as structural support.

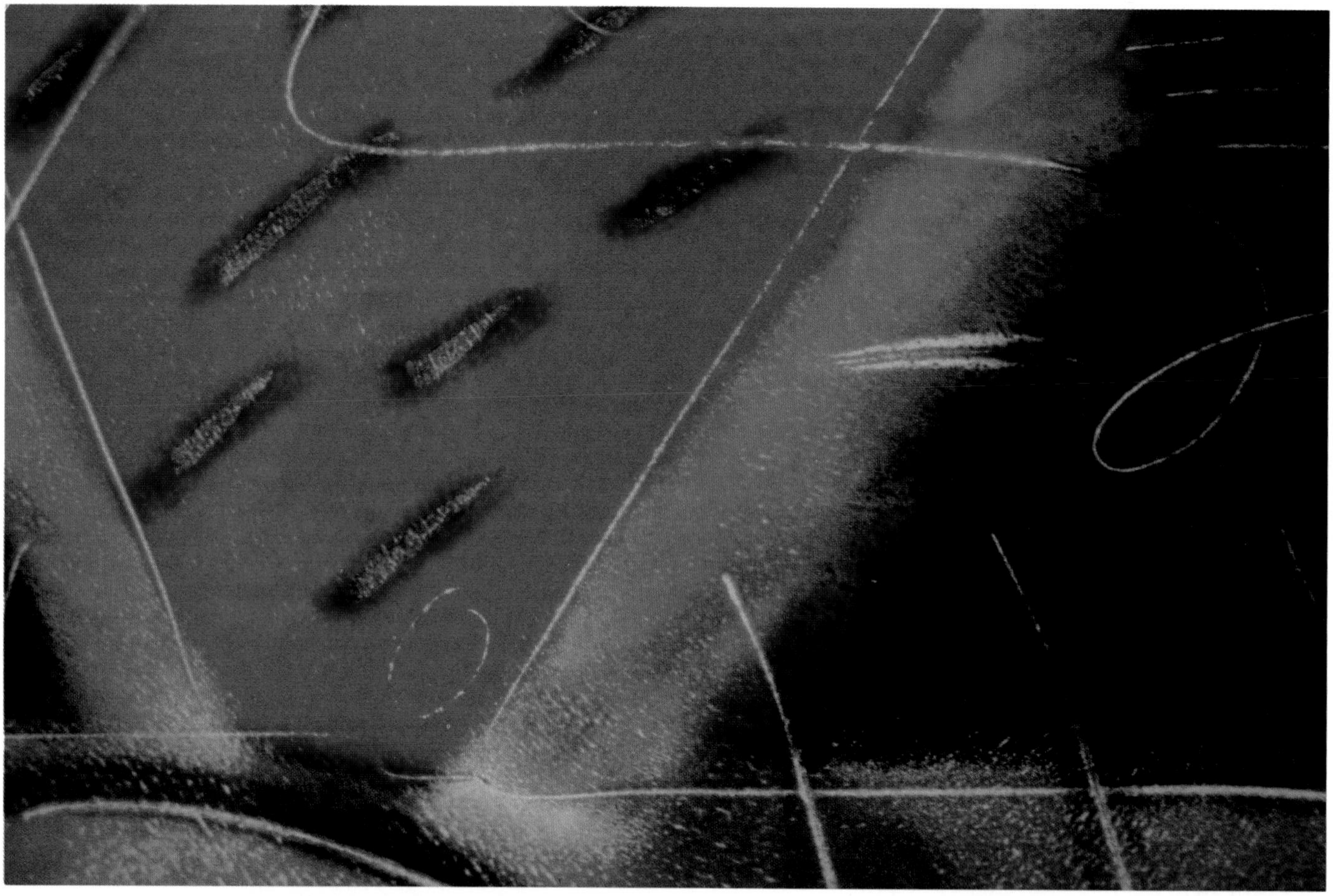

CHAPTER FOUR

Glass enamels are highly fluxed colored glasses that have been ground into fine powder. Their compositions vary depending on the fluxes and coloring oxides present when they are manufactured. An enamel has a melt and flow point lower than the deformation temperature of the base glass to which it will be applied.

The first known enamels used on glass historically were black and brown shades used to "stop out" a certain amount of light from passing through the glass. Enamels are not known to have been used to any great extent until the sixteenth century. By the mid nineteenth century opaque enamels were used extensively for painting "centres" with birds and landscapes in realistic coloring.

Emile Galle, in my opinion, took the application of colored enamels on art glass to its finest form in the late 1800's. In a paper submitted to the jury of the Paris Universal Exposition of 1889 he described some of his achievements and his goals. He reported the development of translucent enamels, new at the time, that were distinct from enamels used in stained glass. "The advantage of these translucent enamels is that they offer complete satisfaction to the eye, whether the pieces are examined in reflected or against refracted beams of light." He stated as one of his goals at that time "to extend the techniques for enriching glass through vitrifiable colors and enamels. New enamels."

When looking at Galle's work, one realizes how successful he was in accomplishing this stated goal. His work stands supreme in the field of enameling. Galle's enameling techniques were made enormously difficult by the variations in coefficient of expansion of different batches of glass. Glass artists today, approaching the same goals Galle had, face the same problems. Very few enamels are available today that do not adversely effect the light refractive properties of glass, and the coefficient of expansion of enamels must be adjusted to "fit" each particular glass.

Light enters through the surface of glass, and leaves through the surface of glass, often the same surface. Glass reflects light off its surface as well, that point where the atmosphere and the glass meet. The character of the glass surface, its texture or lack of it, is the most important aspect in its appearance. I see no reason to make it opaque with enamels, so for the most part, this chapter is about transparent and translucent enamels.

The majority of enamels produced today are for coating cast iron, applying to copper or steel, or for the decorating and labeling of commercial container glass. Enamel glasses are melted in crucible furnaces raised above ground level. The crucible contained in the furnace has a hole in the bottom that is plugged during the melting process. When a full melt is reached, the plug is removed, or in some cases the plug is made of glass and melts, and the glass drains from the crucible into water. This glass is referred to as glass enamel frit. The frit is ground and ball milled to a very fine powder. These powdered enamels range from 80 mesh to 600 mesh in size.

Opposite page: Detail of Elizabeth Mapelli's enamel work.
Detail, "Phoenix Fire Department", 24"x24" screen & enamel panels, Elizabeth Mapelli.

Enamels for metals contain large amounts of lead and potassium in order to facilitate low melting temperatures. They also have high expansion. The largest user of enamels for glass is the container industry, which uses enamels for labeling and decoration, for example, soft drink bottles and decorated glass tableware. These low-fire enamels can be silk screened onto glass and fired in a continuous lehr without deforming the original glass container. These enamels are usually lower in coefficient of expansion than art glass.

The processes used by industry are consistent. Specific enamels with coefficients of expansion lower than the base glass are used because they shrink less than the base glass, so will be more durable, because the surface is under compression.

For most applications in the art world, the high coefficient of expansion of metal enamels or the low coefficient of expansion of labeling enamels is not desirable. There is a great difference between applying an enamel to a round container in small amounts and consistent thickness, and spreading heavy, thick layers over a 2' x 3' piece of float glass for a wall tile. Therefore, unless the manufacturer has specifically formulated the enamel for art applications, its formula must be modified. It must be altered differently for float glass than for Bullseye, since these glasses have distinctly different coefficients of expansion.

ADJUSTING COEFFICIENT OF EXPANSION

It is a good practice for glass workers to make or adjust their own glass enamel colors. An advantage can be gained in knowing that the enamels fit the base glass and that pigment percentages can be changed without sacrificing permanence or density of color. The common practice of applying a thin coat of enamel on glass, in relation to the thickness of the parent glass, is the primary reason most enamels on the market made for glass don't cause compatibility problems with most commercially available glasses. Using a moderate application of enamel, or sandwiching the enamel between two glass blanks, may keep an enamel from crazing off the surface, but it does not change the compatibility problem, if there is one. *If an enamel is not compatible, it is not compatible.* As the size of a piece of work increases or thickness of enamel application increases, the chances of an enameled piece breaking due to incompatibility are greater.

When mixing two materials (enamels and fluxes) or two enamels of different coefficient of expansion, the resulting combinations will have a coefficient of expansion different than either of the original materials and proportional to the coefficient of expansion of the materials combined, but not by simple mathematical formula. A simple line blend of two enamels of different coefficient of expansion, adding the higher coefficient of expansion to the lower coefficient of expansion, should produce enamels of progressively higher coefficient of expansion...and it usually does. However, when adding a simple compound into a complex structure, many complex reactions may take place. One example might be interrupting a eutectic. A eutectic is a mixture whose melting point is lower than any other alloy or mixture of the same ingredients. Some enamels are formed loosely around eutectics. Making additions to this network does not modify it in a purely linear fashion.

Enamel testing is exacting work. Thanks, Dan, for doing all of the line blends!

Our line blend was carried out using volumetric measurement rather than weight. To find the ratio of flux to enamel, we added 1/8 tsp. flux to 9/8 tsp. enamel, then 1/4 tsp. to 1 tsp., then 3/8 tsp. to 7/8 tsp., etc. This results in 10, 20, and 30 percent additions of flux, respectively with the proportions mentioned above. The enamel and flux combinations were mixed by grinding in a mortar and pestle, then sifted. One and one fourth teaspoons of the sifted mixture was placed on a 3" x 10" piece of base glass, graduating the density from light to very heavy. After firing, the samples were cut from end to end and viewed with a polarimeter.

The results of these tests, carried out in our studio, were fired to 1350° F and are as follows.

THOMPSON ENAMEL TRANSPARENT	THOMPSON CALCULATED EXPANSION	ALL ADDITIONS BY VOLUME			
		GLASS BRIDGE	LEAD MONO-SILICATE	TE 426	TE 2020
Light Blue 961	58.33	20%			
Med. Blue 963	61.66	20%			
Cobalt 944	61.0	20%			8%
Amber 973	53.33	20% 1st 5% 2nd			4%
Pink 964	63.33	20%	25%		
Yellow 808	60.66	No Flux Addition Necessary			
Turquoise 279	58.0			10%	25%
Green 1250	59.33			10%	30%
Green 1257	61.66		30%		3%
Green 1218	62.33	Bad	Bad	Bad	Bad
White Opal 1229	61.0				3%
Pink Opal 1295	60.0			10%	30%
Red Opal 1295	57.66	20%			

When making line blends from different batches of Thompson enamels, we found an inconsistency in the C.O.E. of enamel batches of the same color. An example is Amber 973. A first batch required the addition of 20% glass bridge (a ground lead glass acquired from Ed Hoys), while a second batch of 973, acquired three months later, only required a 5% addition. This discrepancy is most likely due to a difference in melting time to which enamels were originally subjected.

We also tested Drakenfeld Versa Color 85 to see how it "fit" over L.O.F. plate glass with a coefficient of expansion of approximately 87. Versa Colors are soft enamels and were fired to 1150°F. The first problem we encountered was an inability to sift the very fine enamels through a screen. The enamel powder is so fine that particles stick to the screen, clogging the openings. To compensate for this, we mixed the Versa Color with Rouche clear #2222, 50%-50% by volume. This flux is approximately 80 mesh, and should be ground a little finer with a mortar and pestle while mixing with Versa Color. The very fine Versa Color coated the large grains of clear, making it easier to sift the fine enamel. The results were very consistent, showing slight but equal stress on all tests. I think Versa Color 85 has great potential as an art glass enamel because of its consistency.

It is very important to test all new batches of enamels before applying them to any architectural job where the work will be mounted overhead. It is just as important that your studio firing schedule is the same for commission work as that used for testing. Enamels can change when firing schedules are lengthened.

Enamel on float glass, by Dan Ott, 20" x 26". The texture was created by fritting plate glass in water, then rolling the wet frit in dry, powdered enamels.

KAISER SUNNYSIDE MEDICAL CENTER
Kaiser Sunnyside Medical Offices
FIRST FLOOR PLAN AND ELEVATOR LOCATIONS

APPLICATION

Enamels may be applied to glass by five basic methods. Each method results in a specific style and will produce an image distinctly its own. These application techniques are sifting, painting, spraying, printing and trailing.

Thompson and Drakenfeld are the manufacturers of most of the colored enamel made for glass. The coefficient of expansion of their enamels must be changed to match the parent glass, if other than very thin applications are intended. When discussing application methods in the following text, we will assume that those adjustments have been made.

Sifting produces soft edges, fuzzy lines, and is one of the best ways of blending color. In the dry-to-dry method the powdered enamel is placed in a small hand held sifter. The sifting cup is tapped while moving it above the surface of the glass. This is often done over a stencil placed on the glass. When sifted, the enamels drop freely to the surface of the glass and the intensity of color is controlled by the movement of the sifter. Colors are readily blended by sifting one color over another. To get color blends, best results are achieved by sifting successive layers of different colors onto the glass surface, not by mixing them beforehand.

When sifting dry powdered enamel onto the slick surface of glass, it is hard to keep from affecting the design adversely. The slightest touch or scrape from a stencil will create marks that, even if repaired, can be noticed after firing. For this reason, the technique of applying an oil or painting medium to the glass is used before sifting. Yet, the dry enamel on the dry slick surface can be used to advantage. Moving the enamel around the glass surface with a rubber eraser stylus or your finger will cause the powder to build up around the edges of the stylus line, making the color more intense in those areas. If two layers of different colors have been applied, the area will be outlined. Heavy applications of enamel work well using this scrafito technique.

Sifting over lavender oil or a painting medium affords more control of line and shape, but loses some of the soft blending qualities associated with the sifting technique. Lavender oil, squeegee oil or Rouche's painting medium #270 are applied to the glass with a brush, stamp, or silk screen. Mixing a small amount of dye into your oil or medium will make it easier to see on the clear glass. The enamel is sifted over the tacky medium, the glass is tilted and excess enamel is dumped off. If the medium is allowed to dry between applications of different colors, fine detail is possible. The surface may be scratched or textured in the usual ways, achieving a crisper line than when the glass is dry. Thick applications are difficult to produce using this technique.

Painting on of enamels requires mixing them with a liquid or carrying agent. Water and alcohol, water and gum, or various mixtures of oil and other materials are used. The enamel medium is important because of its flow properties, its drying properties and its firing characteristics.

Opposite page: 6" enameled glass blocks, Elizabeth Mapelli.
"Kaiser Permanente", Portland, Oregon, 24' x 3-1/2' & 21' x 3', Elizabeth Mapelli.

Applying enamels over a stencil.

Painting media like Rouche #D1368 water base medium, #8200MB, and #270 were designed for brush application. Some media are water base and others are oil base. When using both on one piece, the resistance of one medium to mixing with the other can offer added control. The finer the enamel is ground, the better it will flow off the brush.

Enameling vertical surfaces and adding intricate detail are two good situations for brushing. Galle's work shows a fine example of applying enamels with a brush. His workers often applied a high fire enamel as an undercoat then, after firing once, added a second coat of enamel that matured at a lower temperature. The second layer was often a different shade and more transparent.

Spraying colored enamels is common in the manufacturing process. There are undoubtedly many spray media available, each with its own character. The important properties of a spray medium are its drying speed and its dry strength. Airbrush is the most often used method of application. The character of airbrushed enamels is most often flat and opaque. Detailed shading is the most outstanding attribute of the technique. Airbrushed enamels are usually applied in thin coats. Shading is done by changing color, not by building up a thicker layer of transparent enamel in one place and not another. Most transparent enamels are not intensely enough colored to create tone change without radical thickness differences.

Most enamels should be ground finer than their manufactured state before being used for airbrushing. Four hundred mesh and finer is recommended. Grinding can be done by adding a small amount of water to the enamel and mulling on a piece of plate glass. The enamel should then be thinned by adding alcohol and water in a 1:2 ratio until the mixture will pass freely through the siphon orifice. Airbrush cup attachments that allow the liquid to gravity feed work well and don't clog as often as siphon feed airbrushes.

Enamel on float glass, by Dan Ott. Trailed lines of dark blue glass were made by melting float glass with 1/2% cobalt carbonate in a crucible, before forming the lines, to achieve compatibility with the base float glass.

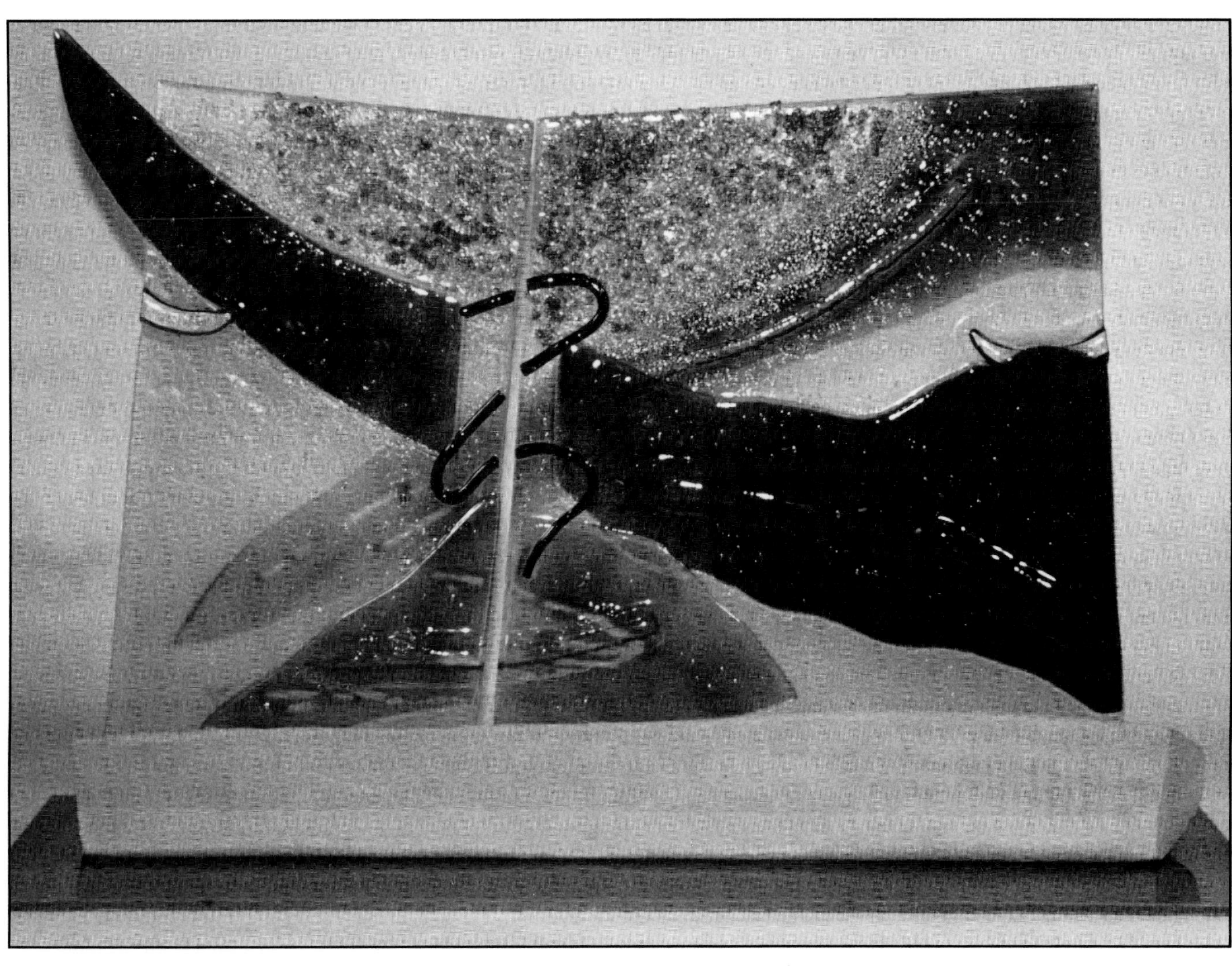

Seventeen-inch platter by Michael Higgins, pre-fired enamels on window glass.

Printing is done with enamels using many of the processes used in the printing trade. For example, enamel is rolled onto an excised design, then pressed against a glass surface. The application is thin and must be done with opaque enamels, which alter the character of the glass. Silk screen can be much thicker.

Silk screen application can be used for making an enamel flashed glass. In the early 1940's Michael and Frances Higgins didn't have available to them compatible glass. They chose to work with window glass and use enamels silk screened over the entire surface to make their own colored glass. The 2' X 3' sheets of glass were fired in a continuous belt glass decorating lehr, to mature the enamels.

At that point, the Higginses had essentially created their own flashed glass with enamels. The sheets could be scored on the non-enameled side and broken as usual. The enamel glass edge remained smooth. When stacking for fusing and slumping (they often do both in one firing), the Higginses sandwich the enamel surfaces between the layers of glass. The first blank is placed enamel side up. Smaller design pieces are placed on top, some enamel to enamel, others enamel up. Then the entire construction is covered with a second blank of the same size, but with the enamel side down.

Where the enamel surfaces touch during firing they change color or intensity, becoming a mix of the two colored enamels. Because the design elements are sandwiched between two full blanks, air is trapped around the design. This keeps the enamel on the top blank from touching the bottom, thereby outlining the shape in the color of the enamel on the top blank. This method also creates a continuous bubble or a bubble pattern within the glass. Many variations of this technique are possible.

One such technique is trailing on top of the fired enamel sheet before covering it with the second full blank. Frances Higgins uses a stylus for trailing that she developed after many years of experimentation. To make the stylus she heats the center of a 6" X 3/8" Pyrex tube in a torch flame, slowly drawing the tube apart to make the mid section narrower. The glass tube is broken in the middle, making two eyedropper-shaped tubes. (An eyedropper can be used as a stylus, but the opening is a bit large for controlling the flow.) The small end is sanded flat and a rubber bulb with a small hole drilled into its side is attached to the opposite end.

By holding a finger over the hole in the bulb, enamel the consistency of cream, can be drawn into the stylus. When your finger is removed from the hole in the bulb, the enamel will flow at a constant rate, controlled by the viscosity of the liquid enamel and the size of the small stylus opening.

The trailed enamels should be allowed to dry slowly before being covered with a second glass blank. The trailed design will trap air inside anywhere lines come back on themselves, enclosing a space. This blank with the trailing design can be fired to maturity before it is covered with a second blank.

Trailing is a good technique for applying transparent enamels thickly, while achieving control with a 1/8" to 1/4" line. If large areas are to be filled or a large multiple-colored drawing created, add a small amount of gum arabic to the water (1:40) before mixing in the enamel. Let trailed lines of one color dry before adding an additional color. In any area surrounded by an already dry line, the fill-in color can be easily floated on without fear of its going outside the outline.

Opening the kiln is often necessary to get a visual indication of whether enamels have matured.

FIRING ENAMELS

Enamels for glass are classified as either soft or hard, depending on the temperature at which they mature. Firing temperatures for soft enamels range from 1000° F to 1200° F; firing temperatures for hard enamels range between 1200° F and 1450° F. The base glass, that is the glass on which the enamels are being fired, must become chemically active in order to create a permanent bond with the applied enamel. Bullseye glass becomes active at approximately 1100° F, while float glass becomes active at 1300° F. Therefore, a soft enamel would not adhere as well to float glass as it would to Bullseye glass. But a hard enamel could be applied to float glass and a soft enamel applied over the hard enamel, in a second firing, and no permanence would be lost.

Successful firing of enamels requires a great deal of practical experience. Many old timers fire using only visual feedback, rather than temperature readings. There are a few general rules to follow to achieve the desired results in firing enamels.

1. Some enamels turn glassy at 800° F, but are not mature.The visual indicators alone would lead you to underfire and may not be adequate. If other enamels are present in the same firing, a comparison can be made between slow and fast fluxing enamels.
2. Heat work is more effective in maturing enamels than temperature alone. Soft enamels fire best when held at 1100° F for 15 minutes, rather than firing fast to 1150° F.
3. An excess amount of binder or the wrong binder can be the cause of frying or bubbling. Too much gum!
4. Overfiring enamels may cause bubbling and/or loss of color. Whether or not enamels are "overfired" can be a matter of preference in achieving the desired results.
5. Enamels boil and lose fluxes as gasses at lower temperatures than the base glass. Enamels held at elevated temperatures for long periods of time will lose fluxes and change in coefficient of expansion.
6. If the enameled piece is over 18-20" in either dimension, the enamels should be tested on an 18-20" strip.
7. The color of many enamels is affected by firing in contact with the tin side of float glass.

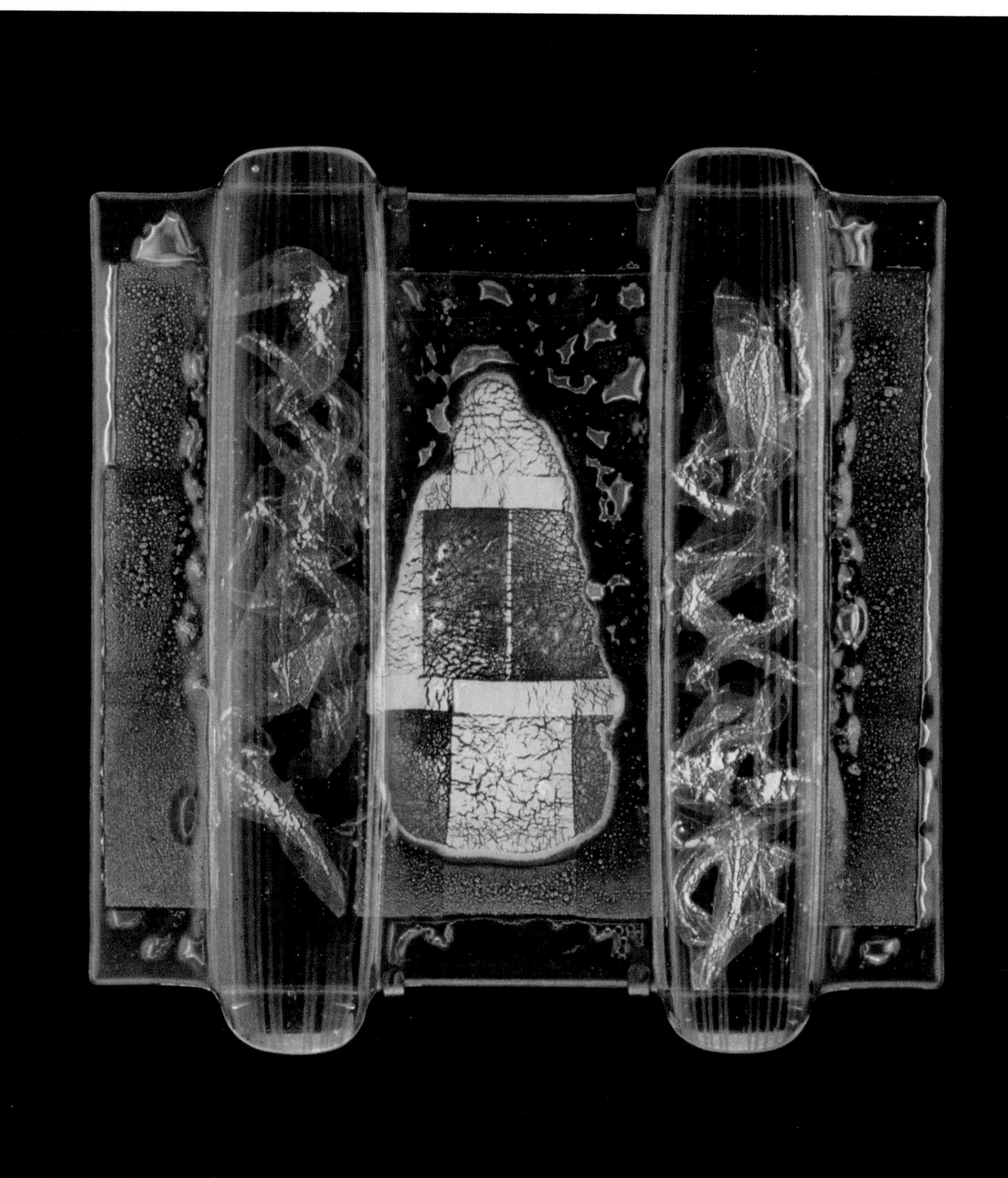

CHAPTER FIVE

Many techniques and materials used in glass fusing do not have a tradition or a body of knowledge to rely upon. Yet the procedures and the materials are very similar to those used in other craft areas. Lusters have been used extensively in ceramics, gold leaf in sign painting, and stannous chloride iridescence has been used by glass blowers. Glass artists must look to these other applications to find information on the use of these materials and then, through experimentation, apply them to glass fusing techniques.

OVERGLAZES

ENGELHARD

Engelhard Minerals and Chemicals Corp. manufactures the Hanovia line of precious metal overglazes used in the ceramic field, as well as the product groups known as Hanovia Lusters, Halo Lusters and Halo Metallics. Other companies often buy Englelhard overglaze products in quantity and relabel them, perhaps making a few additions, and giving them different names. Whereas the Engelhard/Hanovia finishes may readily by found in ceramic supply stores, another line of finishes is marketed by Englehard specifically for glass, and may be a bit harder to find. In any case, either group of products will work well when fired onto glass. For the following discussion all finishes mentioned are assumed to be Hanovia finishes and all will be referred to as overglazes. Firing temperatures are for overglazes made for ceramics.

HANOVIA METALLICS

Liquid Bright Gold is the best known and most commonly used metallic overglaze. It is a solution of gold in solvents and oils. When applied to glass, it is a dark brown oily film until fired. Upon firing to 1200°-1300°F it turns bright gold. Silver, palladium, copper and other metallics all appear approximately the same brownish color when applied, but show their true metallic nature when fired.

LUSTERS

Hanovia lusters allow the user to achieve finishes such as mother of pearl and opal, or one of a series of colored lusters, which, when fired, give transparent colors with an iridescent quality.

HALO METALLICS AND HALO LUSTERS

This is a special group of overglazes that create a halo or ripple effect, when applied in a specific way and fired.

APPLYING OVERGLAZES

Equipment used for applying overglazes should be washed and kept separate. It is not recommended that, even after cleaning, a brush be used for more than one metallic or luster.

Brushing is the most common application technique, although all the Hanovia overglazes can be applied with a stamp, sponge, or sprayer. A fine, camel hair brush works best for applying even coats of liquid overglazes. The oils and solvents that contain the overglaze materials flow easily, so it is advantageous to use a brush that is suitable to the size of the area being painted. For example, a 1/2 inch brush will give a more even application over a large area than a narrower brush.

Opposite page: "Shroud of Cunaxa", 20" x 20", Roger Nachman.

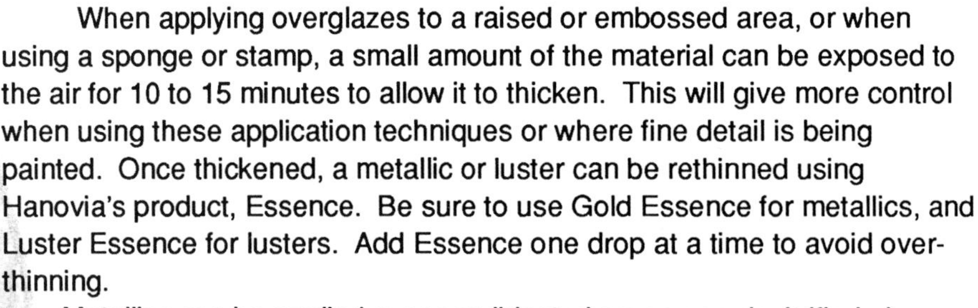

When applying overglazes to a raised or embossed area, or when using a sponge or stamp, a small amount of the material can be exposed to the air for 10 to 15 minutes to allow it to thicken. This will give more control when using these application techniques or where fine detail is being painted. Once thickened, a metallic or luster can be rethinned using Hanovia's product, Essence. Be sure to use Gold Essence for metallics, and Luster Essence for lusters. Add Essence one drop at a time to avoid over-thinning.

Metallics can be applied over sandblasted areas or a devitrified glass surface to achieve a matte finish. For firing over sandblasted areas, blast the glass with a course grit, then fire the piece to just below the fuse point of the glass (1200°F), so that the surface still has tooth. Apply the metallic in a thin-to-medium-thin coat and fire a little lower than usual (50°F lower than the pyrometer reading that gives you full flow with this material).

Clean the glass thoroughly before applying any luster or halo luster. Make sure it is completely dry. Lint, sneezing or cigarette smoke can cause surface imperfection. Moisture in the brush may cause streaks. To avoid this, use Hanovia Brush Cleaner.

When applying Hanovia overglazes, thickness of application and the color of the base glass will affect the final results more than anything else. Gold, platinum, and copper metallics result in various shades of purple, brown, or blue instead of the desired gold, chrome (silver), or copper, when applied on clear or light cathedral glass or when applied too thinly. The same overglazes fired onto darker glass will appear solid gold, chrome and copper when seen in reflected light; these metallics can appear very elusive when the glass is lit from both sides.

The Halo Metallics and Halo Lusters are quite different than Hanovia regular metallic colors. This series gives very special effects when applied to dark opal glasses in the proper way. Three coats of Halo Luster or Metallic are applied over a piece of dark glass, with one to two minutes of drying time between coats. The second and third coats must flow on, since brushing will move (disturb) the layers underneath.

After the last coat has dried, a pointed brush is dipped into Halo Solution and the tip of the brush touched to the dry surface. This will cause a reaction like a rock being thrown into water: the three coats will break into circles, making halo rings wherever the brush has been touched to the surface. Halo lusters and metallics can be mixed, and contrasting colors can be placed over each other. Brush strokes, instead of dots, will create a completely different pattern.

Halo Lusters and Halo Metallics should not be thinned or evaporated because the solvents in these products must be present in exact proportion for the product to work. Always close the container immediately after use. Don't let it stand open while you wait for an area to dry. Halo Lusters work best when the product is first opened. If, over a period of time (three months), you find the halos weakening, it is because some of the material has evaporated. Halo Metallics are dilute concentrations of precious metals. They will always produce shades of purple or blue when applied to clear or light cathedral glass.

Opal and Mother of Pearl lusters give the most effective iridescence over glass. The application should be light and uneven. This can be accomplished by stippling with the brush during application. Applying these lusters over a dark glass or over a pre-fired metallic luster gains best results.

FIRING OVERGLAZES

Let the materials dry in an uncontaminated area, keeping them away from dust, moisture and smoke. Fire to between 1200°F and 1350°F. A longer firing at a lower temperature may be preferable in some instances.

Vent the kiln during the entire firing. Leave all peep-holes open and the lid raised 1/2" to 1". In front loading kilns leave the door ajar and have the piece toward the back of the kiln to avoid thermal shock. Fire in a well vented room or under a hood, as the fumes given off by the luster can affect the brightness of the color. Cloudy or dull lusters are caused by insufficient ventilation or excessive temperature.

Blistering is usually caused by a very heavy application, not by overfiring. As with many other glass practices, in the use of overglazes, well controlled application as well as the most successful firing methods can best be understood thoroughly by experience.

SILVER STAIN

Traditional glass painting techniques employ the use of silver stains. Silver was the first metal used to color glass. Various forms of silver salts, silver chloride being just one, receive an addition of clay to dilute their strength and to add to the spreading, or application, qualities. When fired, the silver is bonded with the glass and the clay modifiers are left on the surface and must be brushed off.

Silver imparts a yellow to amber color to clear glass, depending on its strength. Of course, silver turns a blue glass green, and changes other colored cathedral glasses accordingly, as when adding yellow. When there is a reaction between the silver salts and the base metal used as a colorant in the glass (such as selenium in red), the result may be brown instead of orange. The amount of silver in the stain, as well as the firing temperature, will affect the color. Higher temperatures usually cause a darker color.

Silver stains can be obtained from Rouche in powdered form and are mixed with water. Mixing is usually done with a muller on a flat piece of glass. This material may be applied in all traditional and nontraditional ways. Since, in most instances, firing to 1100°F will cause a reaction between the glass and the silver, it can be applied to free standing dimensional pieces as well as flat glass without distorting the glass.

GOLD LEAF

Using 23 karat gold with fused glass is exciting and somehow imparts a feeling of having "arrived" at a combination of materials that belong together. Glass is a seductive material, and to add a little gold seems to enhance that quality.

Leaf of all kinds comes in books of 25 leaves. Twenty books (500 leaves) make a pack. This is the usual quantity sold. Gold leaf always measures 3 3/8 inches square, silver leaf is usually 3 3/4 inches square, and aluminum and variegated leaf 5 1/2 inches square. Palladium leaf is the same size as gold leaf. All leaf is very thin: from .0000035 inches to .00001 inches. XX gold (23 karat), known as deep gold, is the principal type used for glass gilding by sign painters.

Lemon gold (18 karat), pale gold (16 karat), and white gold (12 karat) are also made for glass gilding, but do not impart a true gold color to glass when fused. Silver leaf is about three times as thick as gold leaf and, when fired, turns the glass a yellow to yellow-green color. Palladium leaf is a silvery metal of the platinum family. It costs more than gold, but stays silver in color and does not turn yellow, when fused. Variegated leaf is a copper alloy. Sometimes called false gold, it comes in many colors, but they all change, when fired with glass, to a bubbly green or green-brown tint.

The basic process of using gold leaf with fused glass is as follows:

1. Clean the glass very well.
2. Apply a sizing medium to the glass so that the leaf will stick.
3. Pick up the gold leaf with a gilding tip brush (came hair) and apply it to the glass.
4. Repeat steps 2 and 3 after drying, until three to five layers of gold have been applied.
5. Cover with clear glass and fire to fusing temperatures.

It sounds easy, but my initial experiments were fraught with frustration. It is very hard to pick up the gold leaf and apply it where you intend for it to lie. Thin areas, where there are only one or two layers of gold do not show gold in color, but wrinkles show where the gold leaf folds. The thicker the gold, the better the color. Firing temperature doesn't seem to affect the gold color. In our studio we found no change from 1300°-1600°F.

A very excellent book, *Gold Leaf Techniques*, by Raymond Le Blanc, discusses the art of applying gold leaf for the sign painting trade. A lot of the book is applicable to the glass artist who wants to study and practice long enough to become proficient at controlling the gold leaf design.

IRIDIZING

There are various solutions of metal salts that can be sprayed on glass while it is hot, that combine with the surface of the glass in a very thin layer to produce a display of lustrous, rainbow-like colors. Stannous chloride is the most successful chemical used for the iridizing process. Other metal salts, such as ferric chloride, may be added to stannous chloride to achieve different colors. The colors produced will depend on the color and the type of glass, as well as how generously the chemical is applied. A good ventilation system and use of an acid vapor respirator are essential, due to the production of dangerous vapors.

STANNOUS CHLORIDE IRIDIZING SOLUTION
1 part by volume stannous chloride crystals
1 part by volume muriatic acid (swimming pool acid)
2 to 3 parts by volume water

Place the crystals in a glass jar and add just enough muriatic acid to cover the crystals. Add enough water to increase the volume to two or three times the volume of the combined first two materials.

The amount of water used depends on what kind of spray apparatus will be used. A glass or plastic siphon sprayer is necessary, since the muriatic acid will eat away at any metal components. A plastic spray bottle is not recommended, since it sprays large droplets and may melt if held too close to the open kiln. I suggest taking your kiln out of the studio into the back yard, using an extension cord, when iridizing is planned.

Open the kiln lid, after turning it off, when the temperature is between 1450°F and 1500°F. Spray a fine mist over the glass. This may take 10 to 15 seconds. Close the kiln and turn it back on for a few minutes to even out the temperature of the glass before annealing. Electrical heating elements are reputed to have their life shortened by being exposed to this acid solution, but I have not personally experienced this.

Wet down the area around the kiln before and after the iridizing spray application. In this way, the very small amount of muriatic acid overspray will be diluted. If this process is going to be used often, construct a properly controlled venting system that allows the containment of overspray.

Thermoluster is supposedly a non-toxic, organic solution, used by glass companies to produce an iridized surface on glass. It is more flammable than the stannous chloride solution, but is sprayed on at a much lower temperature. Good results can be achieved when the glass is 800°F. It is not corrosive to metals, and may be sprayed through inexpensive electric spray guns. This is the solution used by Spectrum and Armstrong glass companies to create their iridescent sheet glass; Bullseye Glass uses stannous chloride. Thermoluster burns off of glass at fusing temperatures. Therefore, glass iridized with this solution will lose the surface effects when re-fused.

Use a good exhaust system when working in a confined space; better yet, work outdoors. Wear an approved respirator and be very careful not to have any red hot material come in contact with the spray. Thermoluster is manufactured by Engelhard Minerals and Chemicals Corp.. It can only be purchased in large quantities and is provided with an accompanying materials safety data sheet.

CHAPTER SIX

Design Technique

Glass technology, the knowledge of basic glass science and forming methods is, and should be, essential to the present day studio glass movement. I think there is a good deal of misunderstanding when it comes to technology and "technique". Whereas glass technology is available to all sincere students of the material, technique is, unfortunately, often considered to be the sole property of an individual. In my view, technique is the application of glass technology. That is, when a specific glass is handled a certain way under certain conditions, it will act predictably, in accordance with the physical laws of glass technology. Artists can affect use of line and color in ways that are totally unique to their particular work, but the techniques they employ for handling the glass are implementations of glass technology, available to all.

I am particularly concerned with this mistaken perception of "ownership" of technique, because I find that it is supported indirectly by other phenomenon in our art glass world, to the detriment of the development of the art glass movement and the people who participate in it. Glass fusing artists sometimes find that a particular technique works well for them, and stay with it in all of their work for a while. If these same artists are successfully showing their work on the art gallery scene, their work may become recognizable by its being a result of a particular technique.

Designing on graph paper can facilitate cutting and laying up of cross section designs. Stacking techniques are easily visualized if they are cut across the color design and looked at edgewise. The "zipper" patterns designed by Peter Wendel show two stacking techniques clearly: shingling layers and alternating layers. Peter's process starts by fusing strips of Desag G.N.A. cathedral colors into large blanks. The fused stripe designs that result are cross cut into 3/8" strips and then restacked on their edge. Each restacking process creates a distinctly individual pattern that is pure in color and line, since the colors do not blend, intensify or change in hue when viewed as a cross section of the original fusing.

Opposite page: Fused glass bowl, 19" diameter, Peter Wendel.
Zipper bowl, Peter Wendel.

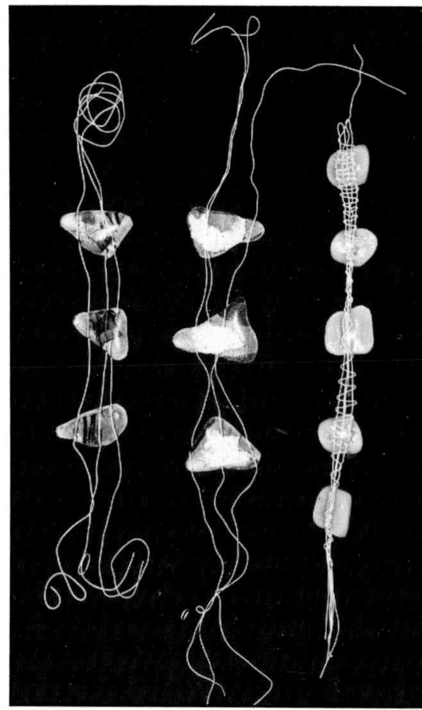

Jewelry by Rika Kiroki. Holes are formed in beads by fusing over copper wire, then stretching the wire to reduce its diameter, so that it will easily slip out of the beads.

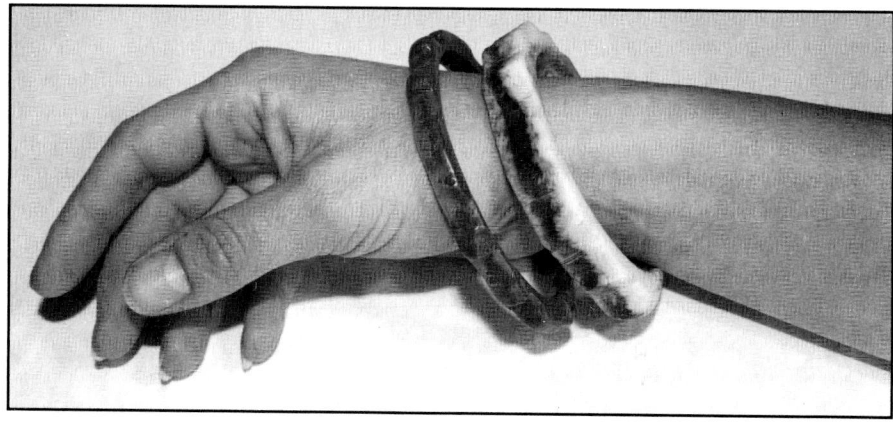

Pate de verre bracelets.

Gallery and shop owners often choose to display the work of only one glass artist who uses a particular process, and tout that artist to their customers as being the sole owners (the implication here is that they are the only authentic producers) of work in that technique area. The unfortunate result is that the gallery owner, gallery artist, glass student, and collector all become convinced that the technique used by that particular artist is sacred, and cannot be explored by others without being counterfeit.

This is particularly disturbing considering that the gallery artist may not be the one who first explored the technique anyway! Regardless of who's art work is best (or if they are equally fine), the artist who is best at gallery hustle will end up famous for a technique perhaps used by many before him.

I repeatedly see my students go out of their way to avoid using a certain technique, because someone of notoriety has gotten a lot of attention for a series of art glass pieces using that technique. They believe that a scientific breakthrough or a new fusing material or larger scale work will give them an advantage in the art marketplace. And it will! My students tell me that big is good and bigger is better. And it is. Technique applied in this way is negative, thoughtless, and shortsighted.

Star Wars bowl by Patrick Lundstrom, using pre-fused design elements. The visual effects of color dimension within the glass is created by affecting the hue, the saturation and lightness of color. Use of these effects gives the finished project a certain depth, suggesting a background and a foreground. Generally, this technique can only be used when over laying a glass transparent enough to show the glass under it, and is most effective in backlit projects.

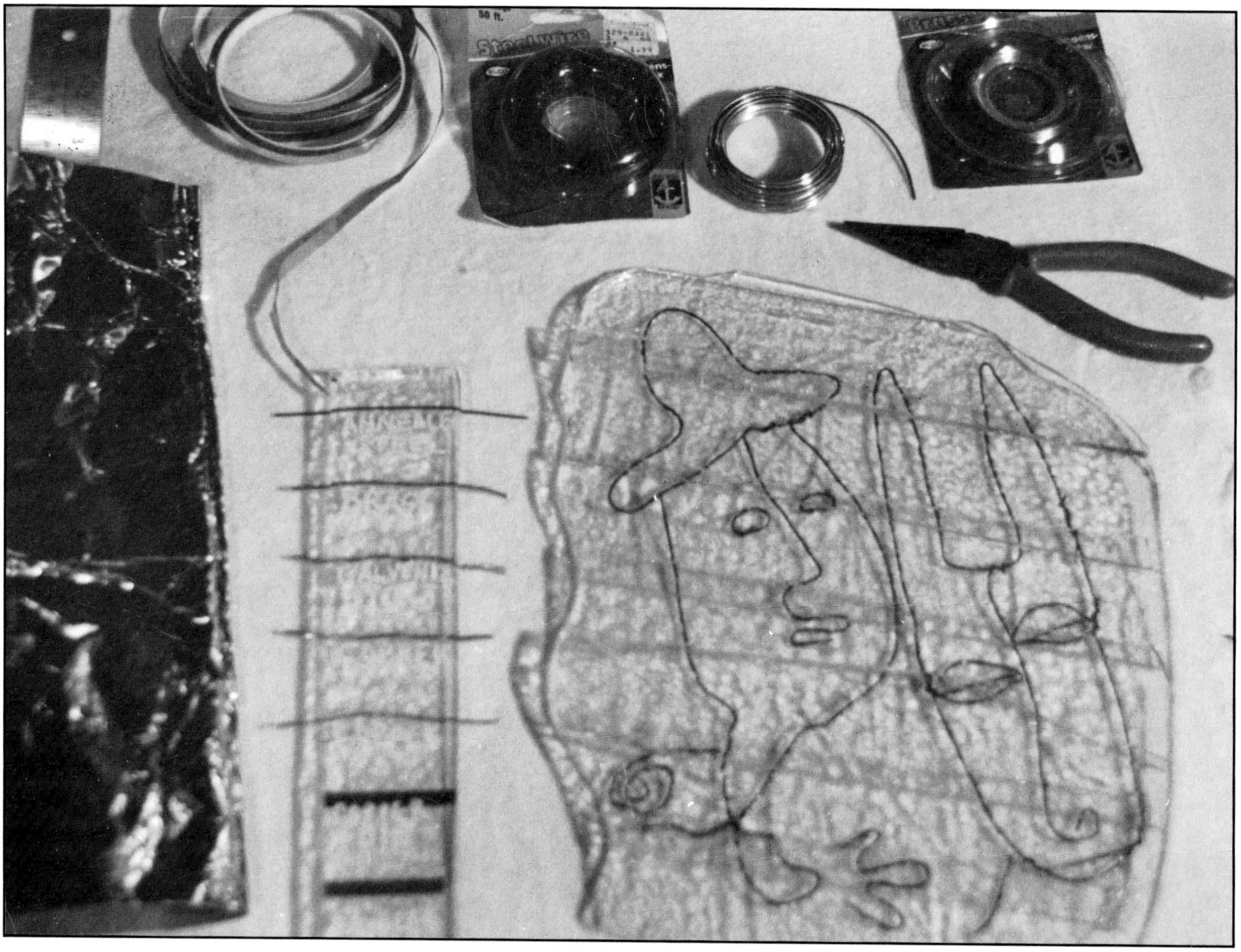

Test tiles resulting from trials of fusing various types of metal wire and foil between glass. In addition to visual results, each material was tested for its compatibility with various glasses.

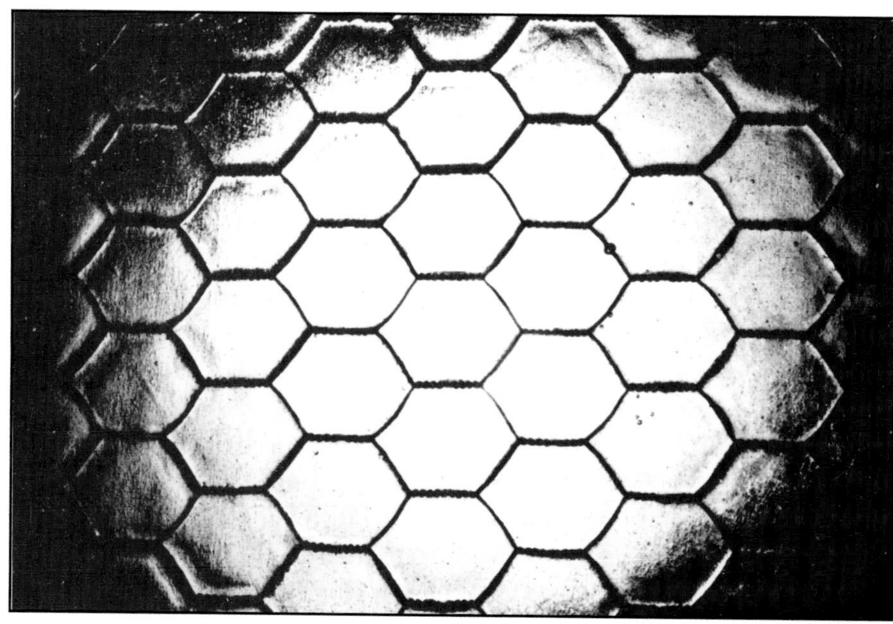

Chicken wire between layers of Bullseye glass.

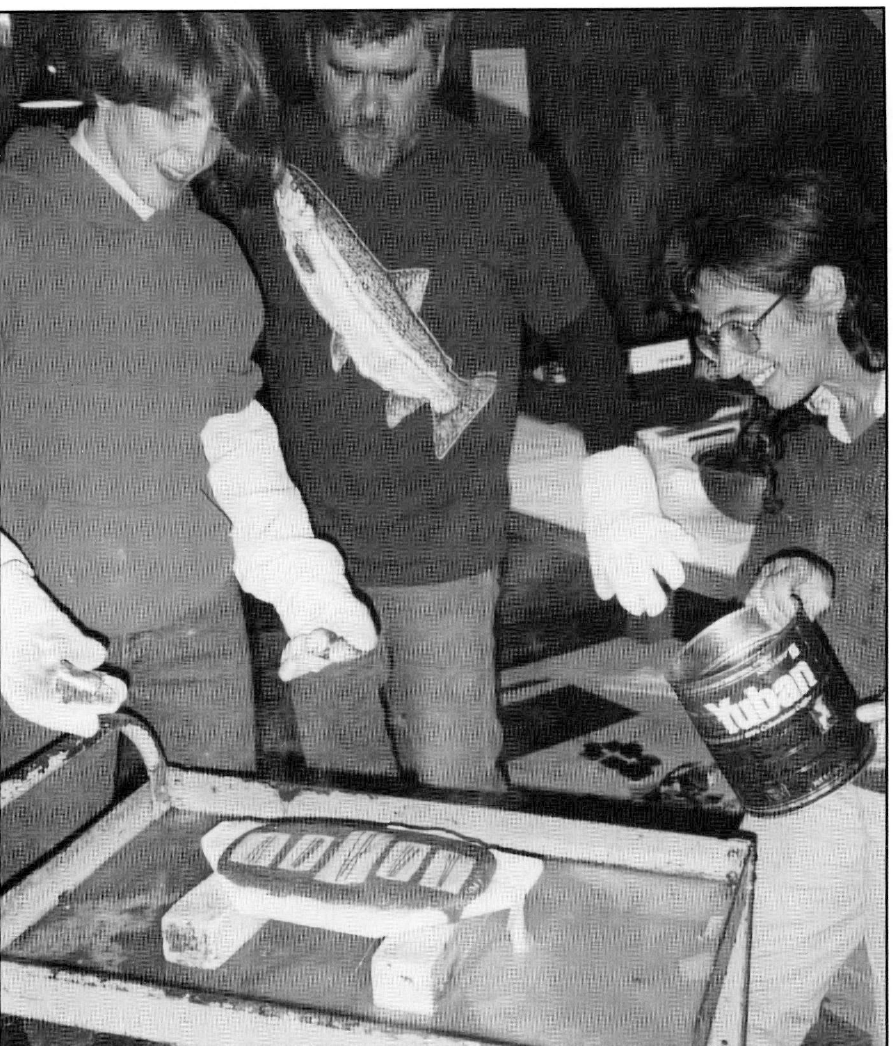

Making crackle glass. Martha pours cold water over a fused tile, removed from a kiln at 1550°F. The glass must be returned to the kiln and flash fired, to fire polish the edges of the fissures created when the surface crackled. Crash cooled to 1300°F, and then annealed for a length of time appropriate to its thickness, the glass will retain its unusual surface texture.

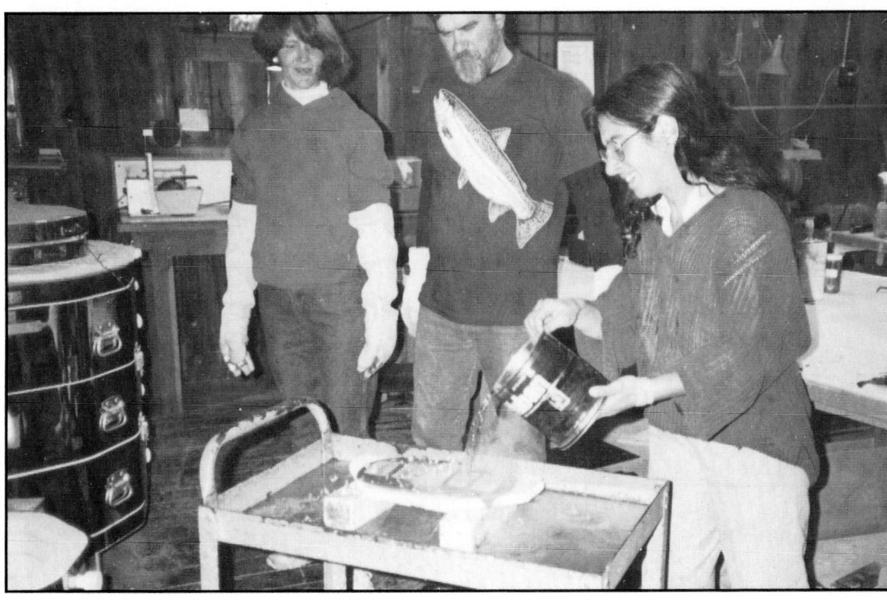

Fused glass tiles, made by Hal Bond, for the platform tub, sink top, and walls in bathroom in Nelson residence, Salem, Oregon. (Photo by Mike Renfrow)

It takes time, money, and practice, and then more money to experiment and develop techniques. But no technique should be held to be exclusive to an individual who uses it, and all technology should be shared.

Technique is developed through the application of knowledge. The eccentricities of a process can only be understood through active participation; it takes practical knowledge to make it work. How many cooks do you know who can just open a book and turn out a delightful meal, if they haven't diligently studied and practiced cooking for years to understand the subtleties of the interplay of ingredients and technique? Technique is developed, not acquired, and to develop it one must practice. If a student of glass technology, as it applies to art glass, shies away from techniques used by well-known artists, that student is denying himself a learning experience and is unnecessarily limiting his glass education. I look at technique as practical knowledge.

In time, as understanding of glass technology, not tricks, becomes prevalent in the contemporary art glass movement, and glass collectors and merchants are exposed to more glass with thoughtful content, it will become apparent that "technique" is not cheap.

Tiles for the expansive kitchen counter (136" x 127"), by Hal Bond, were made of Spectrum and Bullseye glass for the Nelson residence, Salem, Oregon. (Photo Mike Renfrow)

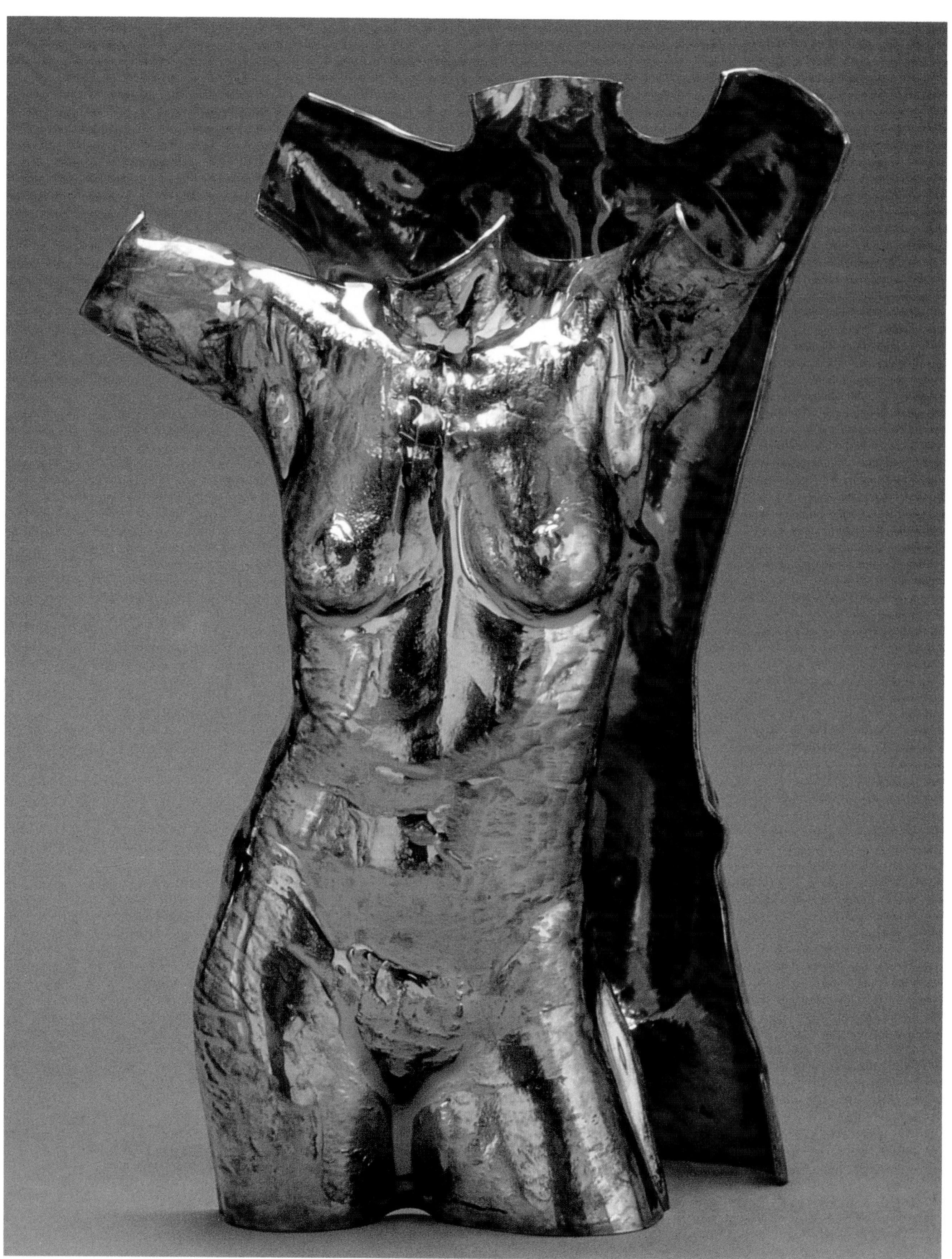

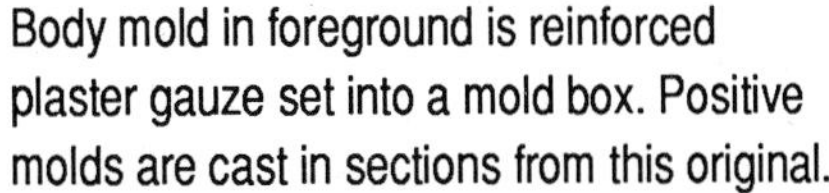

Body mold in foreground is reinforced plaster gauze set into a mold box. Positive molds are cast in sections from this original.

Linda Ethier inspects life size completed piece that has been slumped over mold sections. Mold pieces compress to keep glass from fracturing as it shrinks upon cooling.

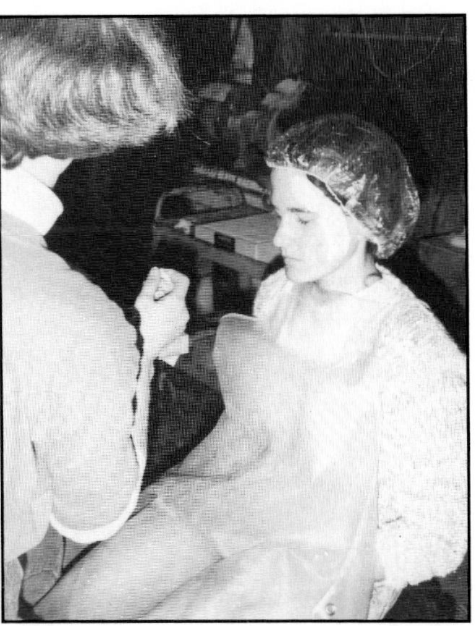

Applying plaster gauze to the face is the first step in making a "death mask". A positive mold is then made by casting a refractory mold material into the hardened mask.

Opposite page: "The He and She of it", 35" x 23" x 20", slumped float glass with metal plating on inside surface, Linda Ethier.

CHAPTER SEVEN

Slumping & Sagging

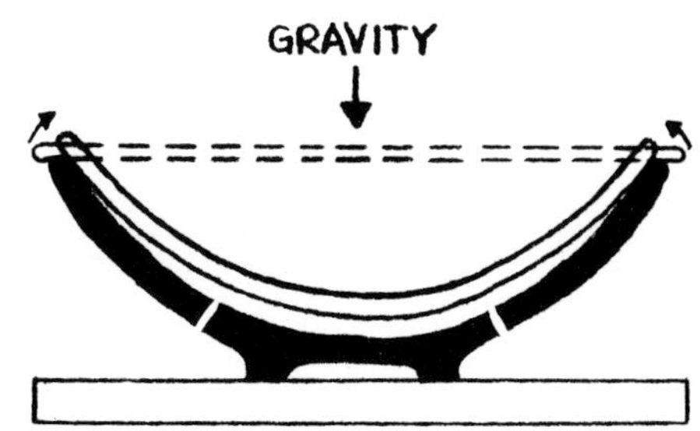

Slumping and sagging glass are processes of the use of heat and gravity to change the shape of a flat tile to a three dimensional form. These terms are similar in meaning and are often used interchangeably, leading to confusion. Because words are tools of communication, clarification of specific terms is necessary.

Slumping is nearly synonymous with sagging, however, slumping usually implies a bending *without noticeable change* in the thickness of the cross section of the glass. By keeping the temperature as close as possible to the fiber softening point (but high enough to allow downward movement), noticeable stretching is avoided.

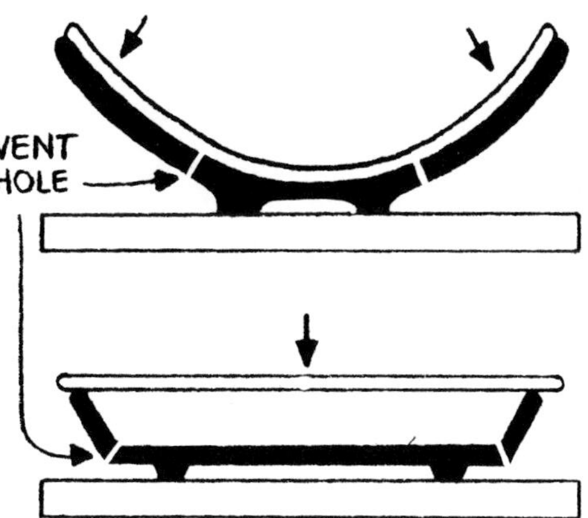

Sagging is the downward sinking of glass, caused by its own unsupported weight as the glass softens when heated. We refer to sagging as a process whereby the thickness of the glass cross section *changes noticeably* due to stretching.

Glasses are often referred to as hard or soft. Harder glasses generally slump at higher temperatures and at a slower rate than soft glasses. Window glass and GNA glass are considered hard glasses. Some Bullseye glasses are hard, such as white, pink opal, and green opal. Others are soft, such as black and most Bullseye cathedrals. This means that different glasses, even from one glass manufacturer, can vary. Spectrum and Wasser glass are relatively soft glasses.

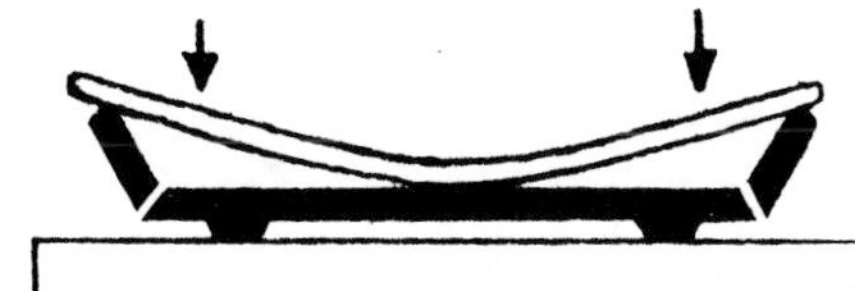

Glass melts or moves when exposed to heat work, not just temperature. A beef roast can be cooked at 400°F for three hours to achieve doneness or at 300°F for five hours to achieve the same doneness. It is heat work that cooks the roast. It is heat work, time and temperature, that should be controlled when sagging or slumping glass.

SLUMPING

When a tile is placed over a mold and fired between 1300°F and 1350°F, the glass will slump and conform to the shape of the mold. Slumping should be done slowly. It is often necessary to slow the temperature rise of the kiln at 1300°F to allow heat soaking of the glass. This will even the temperature across the pre-fused tile, resulting in better, more even conformation to the mold.

Glass slumps first where the most weight is unsupported. Edges that overhang a mold will turn up as the middle sinks down, unless the overhang is great. As the slump progresses, the edges fall and the mold fills. In a square mold, the corners always fill last.

Vent holes are necessary in all nonporous molds. Vent holes should be placed in the areas of the mold that fill last. The center of the bottom always fills first, therefore is not the proper place for venting air trapped between the glass and the mold.

Opposite page: Fused glass deep slumped bowl, 18" diameter, Tim O'Neill.

When a 9 1/4" tile is slumped over an 8-3/4" shallow bowl mold, the four corners of the square tile fold over the outside of the round mold, creating triangular feet on a round bowl. If the triangular areas outside the round mold are not large enough to touch the kiln shelf they will turn back under the lip of the round mold, trapping the mold and making release impossible.

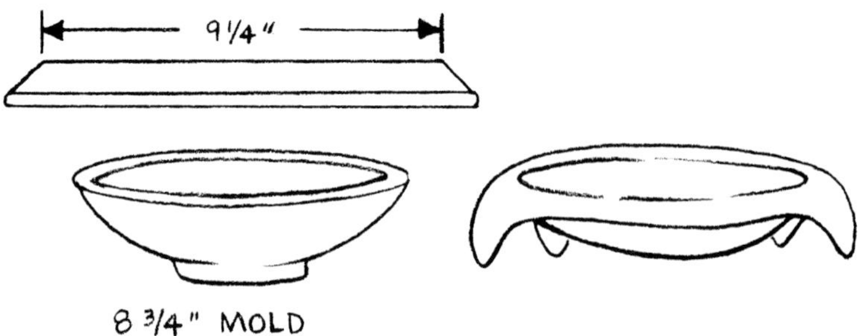

When a tile of the same size, 9 1/4", is slumped into a 12" round mold, the result is quite a different shape, because the tile fits totally inside the 12" mold. Much of the shape of a finished piece depends on the size and shape of the original tile, in comparison to the size of the mold.

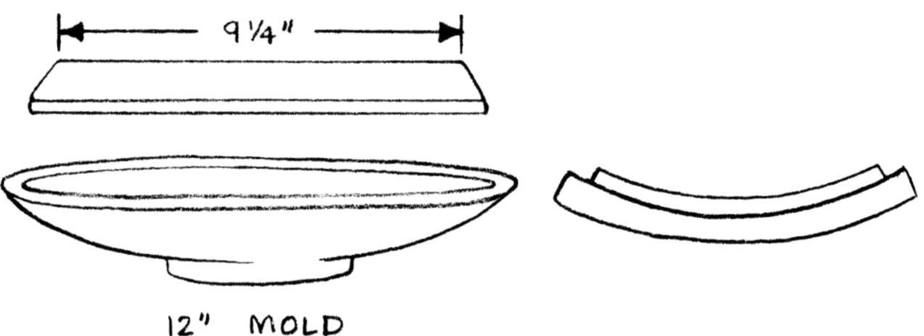

A third shape is created when a 9 1/4" tile is slumped over a 8 1/2" square mold. Since a mold of this shape has corners, more time at slumping temperatures is necessary to allow the glass time to fill the mold cavity, because there is more glass that must fit into a constricted area. These three examples are very basic, but should be observed and understood before trying the use of more complex slumping molds.

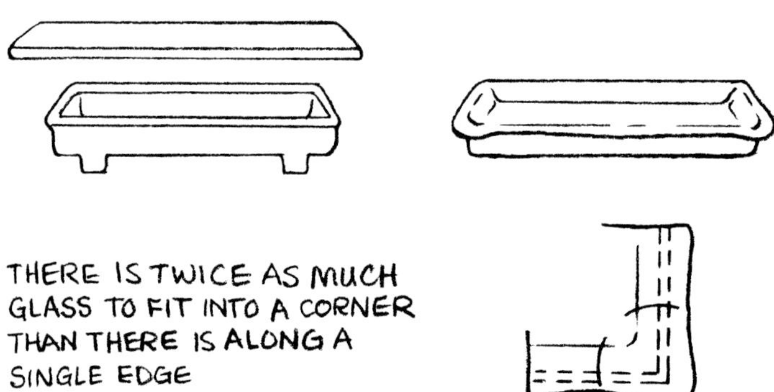

Some slumped forms require the use of more than one mold. A deep bowl is just about impossible to slump in one firing using a single mold. A couple of things are likely to happen when an attempt is made to slump a large circular blank into a deep bowl all in one firing. The blank may stretch more on one side than the other, causing an off-center bowl with one side as much as two inches shorter than the side opposite. Or the glass may stretch on one side and ripple on the other, making an irregular, wavy lip.

To avoid these problems, a series of three progressively deeper and narrower bowl molds are used, in order to maintain control of the glass thickness and shape. To accomplish a deep bowl slump, the first slump is done into a platter mold, the second into a bowl of intermediate depth, and a third into a deep bowl with a flared lip.

Draping glass over a tall form is a slumping process because, even though the glass folds back on itself, it does not change noticeably in thickness. There is a lot of chance and whimsy involved in draping. A blank of the same size, placed over the same mold, will almost never fold and drape the same way twice. There are similarities, but not many duplicates. It is a lot of fun to do a study of the variations, as in the following experiment.

Place a square or circular glass blank, in the kiln, over a metal or ceramic mold taller than one half the width of the blank. Heat the kiln very slowly; it is very easy to thermal shock a piece of glass that is supported only in the center. The glass will first fold in half forming a taco shell, then the two highest edges will fold down dividing the taco shell in half, forming quarters. At times it will fold into thirds and then sixths. Some control is possible by shaping the top of the drape mold.

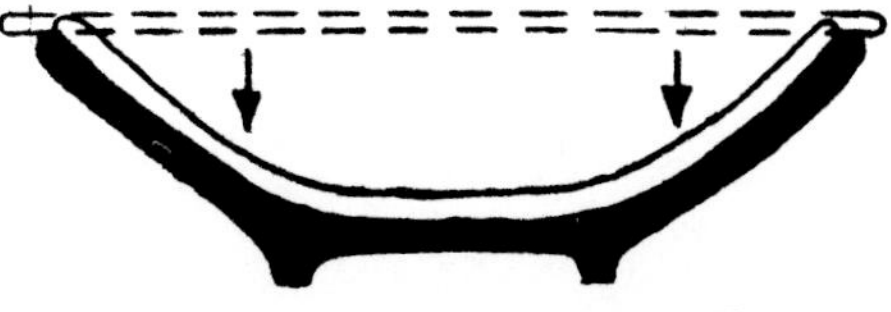

MOLD 1 - FIRST SLUMP

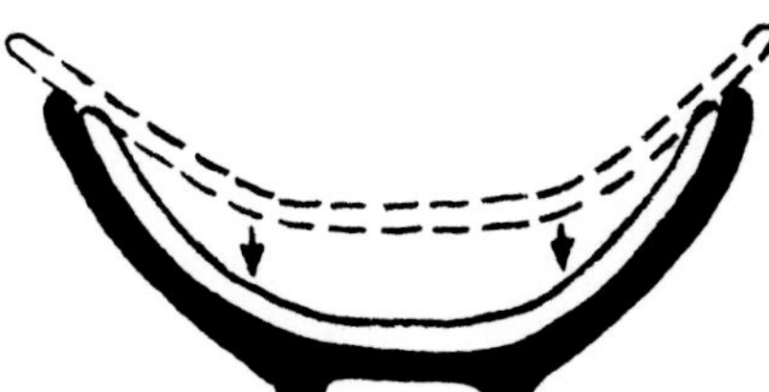

MOLD 2 - SECOND SLUMP

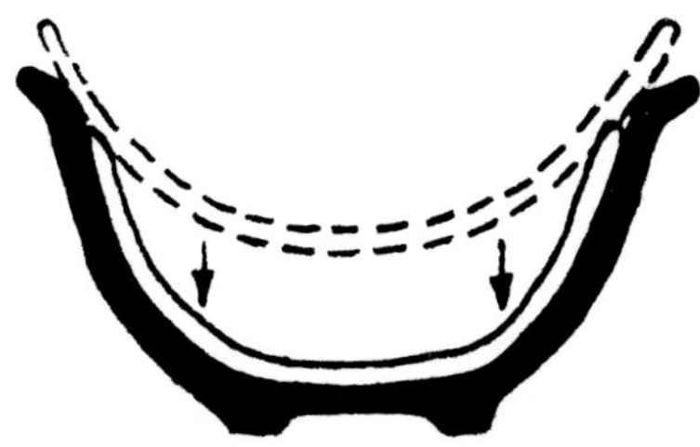

MOLD 3 - THIRD SLUMP

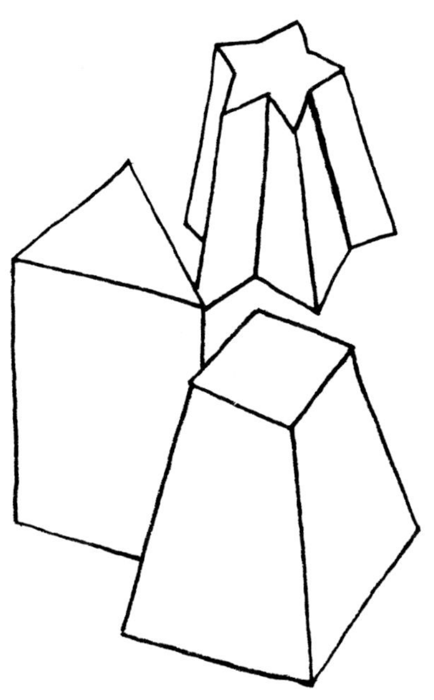

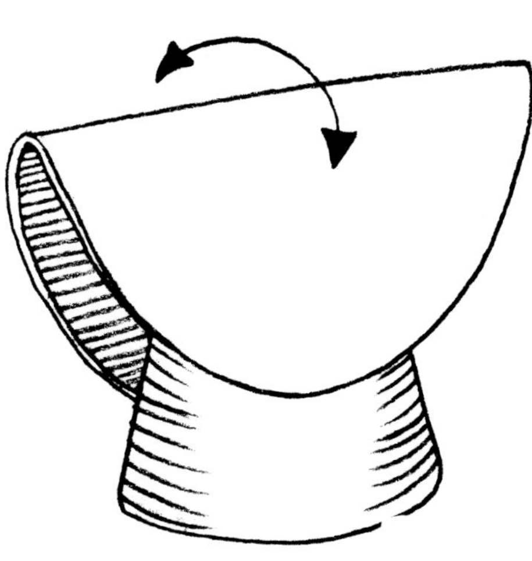

AVOIDING THERMAL SHOCK

When slumping and then annealing a slumped form in (or over) a mold, there are three problematic areas to be aware of. Consider a typical slump: a pre-fused 9 1/4" circle to be slumped into a 9" bowl mold. The circular blank is 1/4" thick and has a design of different colors. It will be fired in a top element fusing kiln.

The first thing to notice is that different colors absorb heat at different rates. Black absorbs heat much faster than white. Secondly, the air trapped between the glass blank and the mold acts as an insulator. Thirdly, if the mold absorbs heat faster (or slower) than the glass, the glass will be affected where it touches the mold. For these reasons, it is important to raise the temperature in the kiln slowly to avoid thermal shock. A rule of thumb is to allow 10 minutes for each one inch of blank width between room temperature and the strain point of the glass. For Bullseye glass this would mean taking approximately 90 minutes for a 9" blank and 120 minutes for a 12" blank, to heat the glass to 900°F, safely past the strain point. This applies to tiles comprised of up to two and a half volumes of glass, ie. two layers plus design pieces.

Glass that has not been fused flat, and has thick and thin textured areas has a greater tendency to thermal shock than does a piece of glass of even thickness. Glass that is supported in the center, such as a mask or a draped lamp shade, has a tendency to thermal shock. Moisture in the mold and uneven mold thickness may cause thermal shock. If any of these conditions exist, add more time to the initial temperature rise.

After the slump is completed there is the potential for uneven cooling during annealing, due to the mold configuration, mold placement, or unevenness in mold material. The most important attribute of a slump mold is that it have even wall thickness.

If the mold has a foot and has been placed on a kiln shelf or the bottom of the fusing kiln, air may be trapped between the foot of the mold and the shelf. This trapped air acts as an insulator and will keep the bottom center of the slumped bowl from cooling at the same rate as the elevated sides. To avoid this situation, place molds on small stilts or broken pieces of kiln shelf to elevate the mold.

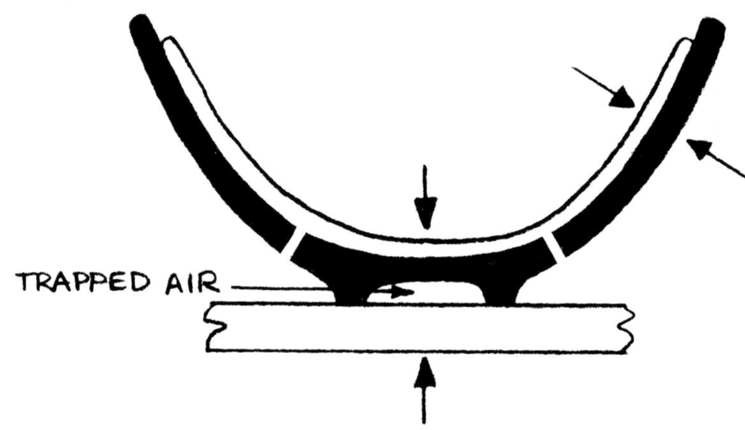

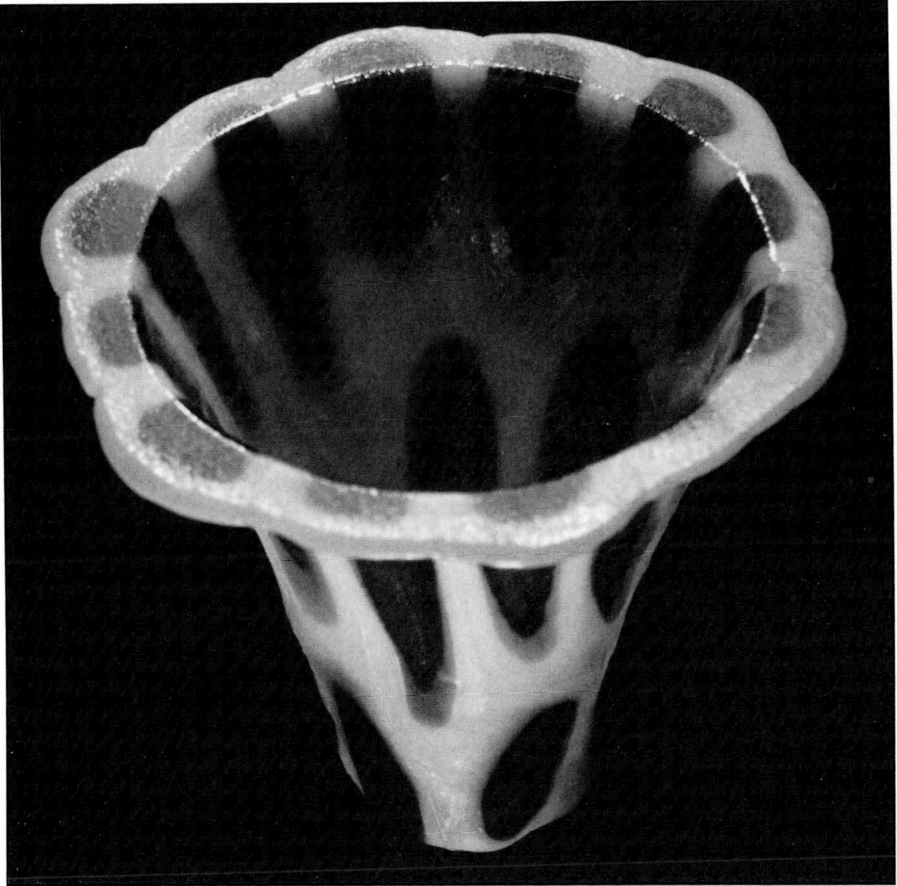

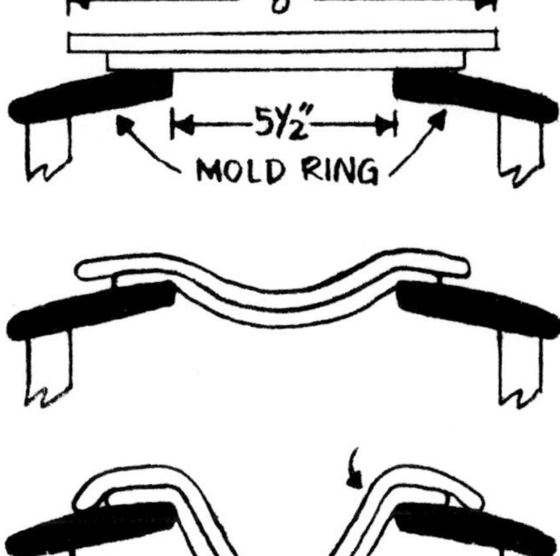

GLASS STARTS TO STRETCH NEXT TO INSIDE LIP

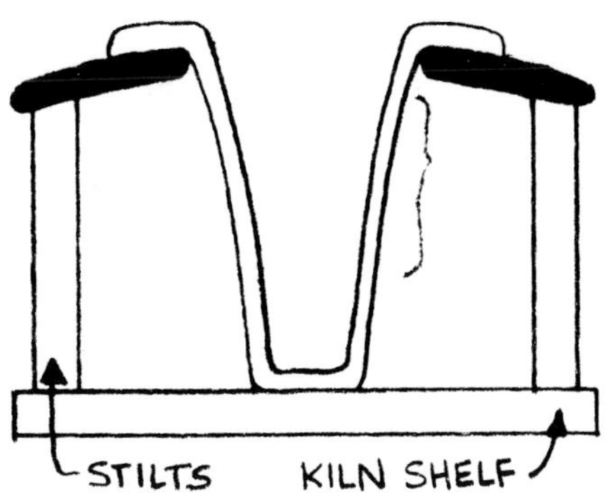

GLASS CONTINUES TO THIN BELOW INSIDE LIP

SAGGING, THE DROP-OUT

The basic "drop-out" glass form is made by sagging two or three layers of glass through the center hole of a donut-shaped mold. This process is often carried out during one firing. The glass blanks placed on the mold, at one time, laminate together (fuse, but not fully) as they sag through the hole in the donut-shaped mold. The glass stretches until it reaches the kiln shelf and flattens, forming the bottom of the vase. There are many variations of this process, some using pre-fused discs and others using more than one hole in the mold.

The shape of a drop-out form is affected or developed by controlling many factors. These are: the glass composition, the rate of the sag, the shape of the opening in the mold, the distance the glass sags before reaching the kiln shelf or kiln floor, and the location of heat sources within the kiln.

The sagging (and slumping) properties of a particular glass are uniquely linked to its composition; glass of a specific composition stretches or deforms under its own weight, as affected by gravity, at a rate and temperature determined by its composition. Bullseye black 0100 and white 0113 slump at different temperatures, approximately 50°F apart. These two glasses also move at different rates; black moves rapidly and white moves slowly. This one example of two Bullseye colors may be extreme, but should point out that even when compatible glasses are used, large variations may exist.

Glass sagging through four flower molds with different sized stem openings. The mold with the largest opening sags first and forms the longest stem.

Window glass (1/8 inch float process glass) sags through a drop-out mold at a temperature 100°F above the sag point of Bullseye and 125°F above the sag point of Spectrum. The slumping properties of a glass are not determined by the coefficient of expansion of a glass but by other characteristics of glass composition.

Therefore, concise temperature information cannot be stated for the drop-out process. In general, the drop-out process is carried out between the temperatures of 1300°F and 1400°F, over a period of 45 minutes after the glass starts to move. The shape and size of the mold as well as the distance of the drop affects the time it will take and the shape of the finished piece.

The temperature at which various glasses start to move or deform also depends on the amount of time spent in reaching that temperature. If GNA glass is heated to 1350°F over a two hour period it will start to sag through a 5 1/2" opening; if heated to the same temperature in 1 hour it will not. GNA will start to sag at approximately 1375°F to 1400°F, if the temperature rise is greater than 20°F per minute. And once it starts moving, it will drop through the mold opening at a faster rate than that of GNA heated more slowly, resulting in a loss of control.

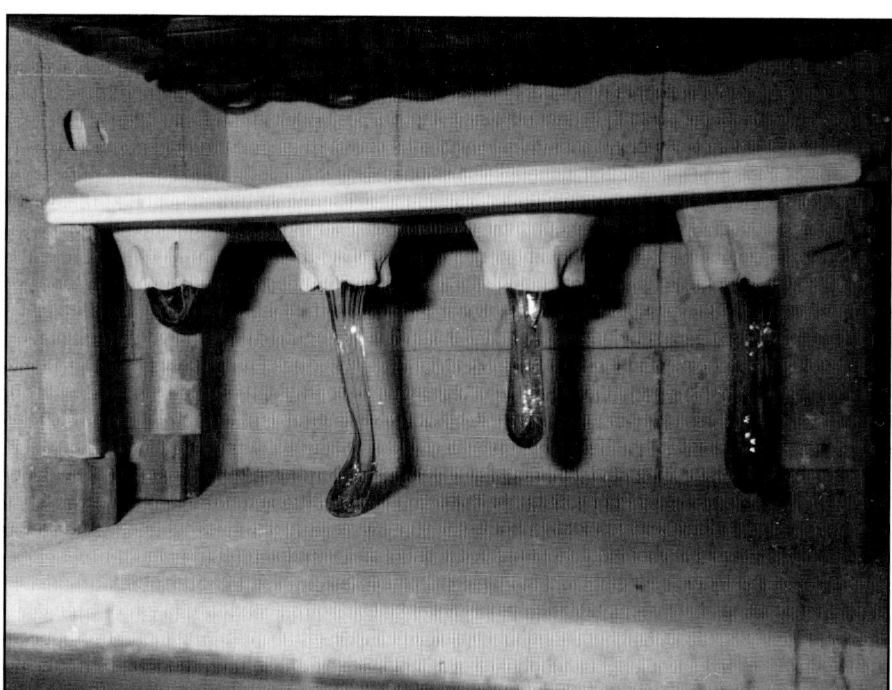

The slower the temperature rise after the glass starts to move, the more control you will have, resulting in a more even wall thickness in the finished piece. The time spent in the slumping zone has the greatest effect in achieving control. As a rule of thumb, a firing rate of not more than 5°F rise in temperature per minute should be maintained after reaching 1200°F. This can be varied depending on the hardness of the glass and the size and shape of the mold.

TOP FIRE

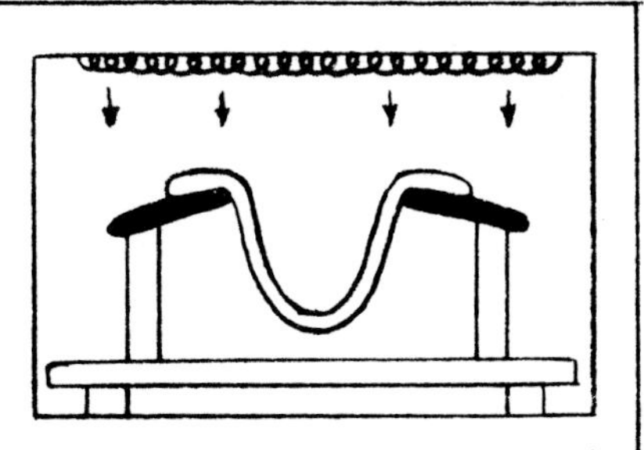

THE GLASS GETS FURTHER FROM THE HEAT AS IT SAGS

SIDE FIRE

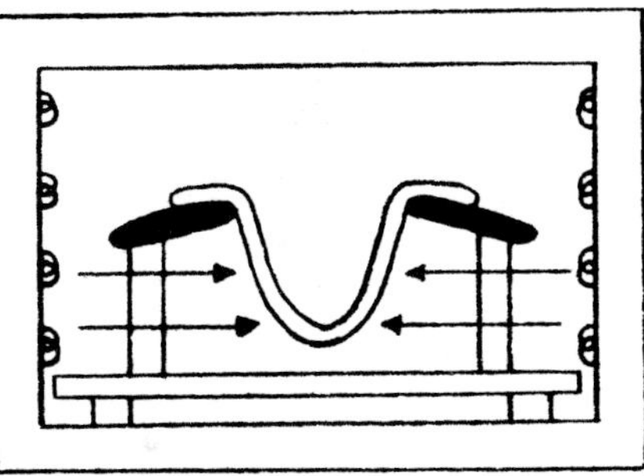

WHEN FIRING DROP-OUTS IN A SIDE FIRE KILN, THE WALL THICKNESS REMAINS MORE EVEN THAN WHEN FIRING TOP FIRE

A top fired fusing kiln is not the best kiln for sagging glass. This can be easily understood once you see the product from different types of kilns. For discussion purposes let's say we are going to slump two 8" glass blanks through a donut shaped mold with a round 5 1/2" opening that has been stilted 6" above the kiln floor. If a top fired kiln is used, all the heat radiation from the top of the kiln heats the glass evenly until it starts to move. As the glass sags through the opening in the mold it moves further away from the heat. The glass closest to the top of the kiln stays hotter and stretches thinner, the thinner glass accepts heat faster and the result is paper thin glass just under the lip of the finished form.

This is not the case when the elements are on the sides of the kiln or on the bottom half of the kiln. A ceramic kiln with two rings (such as Skutt 818), where the elements can be controlled separately (upper and lower elements), is an excellent kiln for accomplishing the drop-out process. As the glass starts to sag, the upper elements can be turned down and the lower elements can be turned up. This heats the glass more evenly as it moves through the opening and drops toward the bottom of the kiln. Many small front-loading kilns are on the market that have elements only on three sides of the kiln. These kilns heat the glass unevenly and often cause the finished form to be off-center and uneven because the glass stretches less on the door side where there is no heat source.

The heat source configuration (position of elements) in the kiln affects control of glass movement. This is not to say that a special kiln is necessary for the drop-out or air mold process. By slowing down the heating rate just as the glass starts to move, control can be gained in any kiln.

Completed sagged form with three bowl shapes, 15" x 22".

A bisque clay slab with three openings is suspended on wires supported from the top edge of the kiln. The lid holds the wires in place. A kiln shelf is placed under the suspended mold.

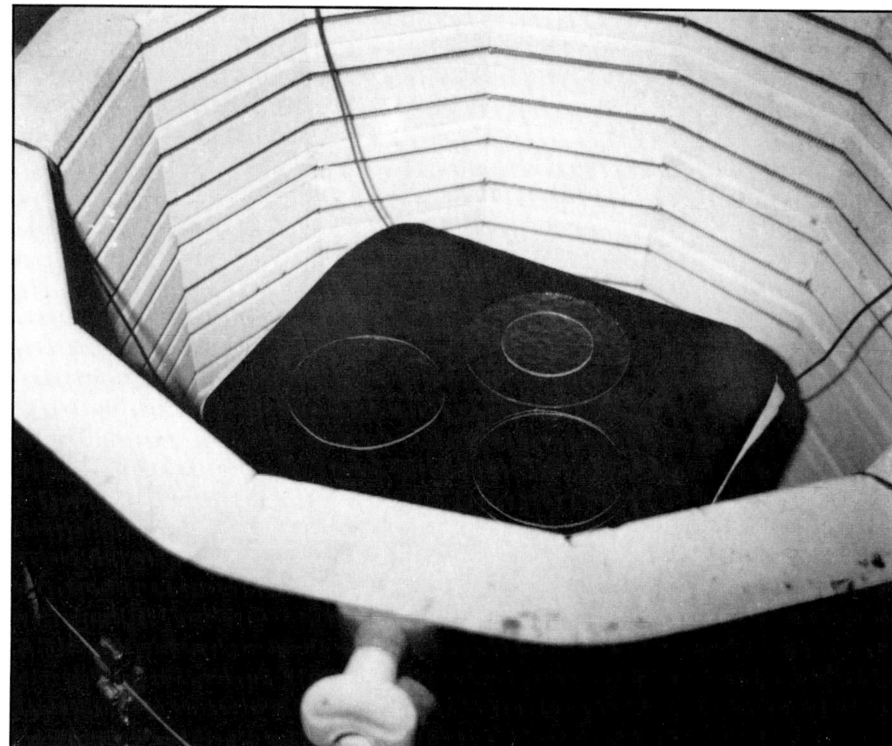

Two layers of glass, with a third layer of cut circles placed on top, covers the suspended clay mold. After the glass has sagged and cooled to 1200°F, the wires are released, lowering the mold away from the glass, to keep the glass from entrapping the mold.

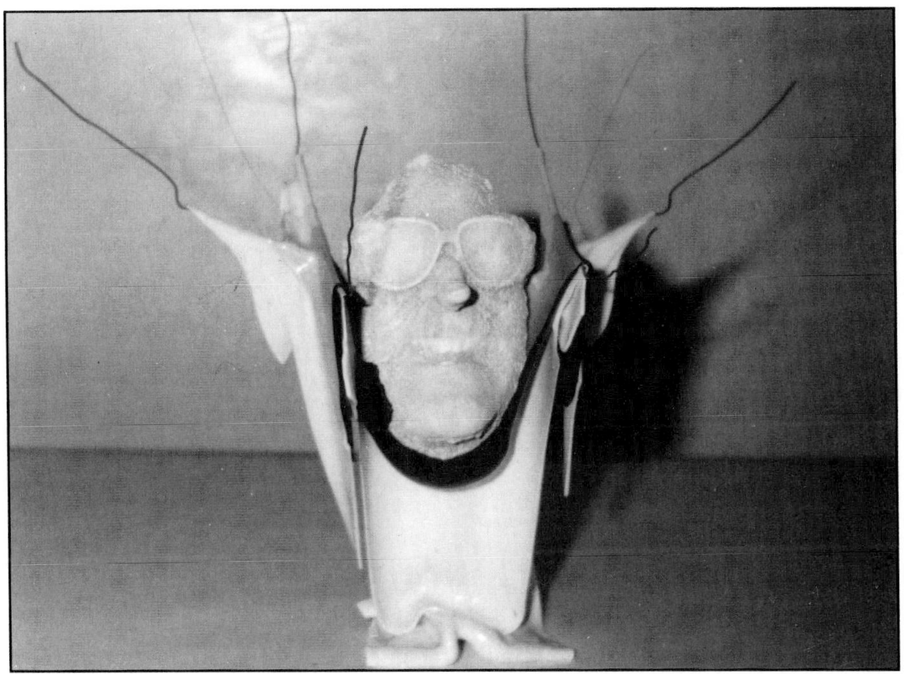

Sagged sculpture with copper wire left in place. Cast face was glued in place after sagging.

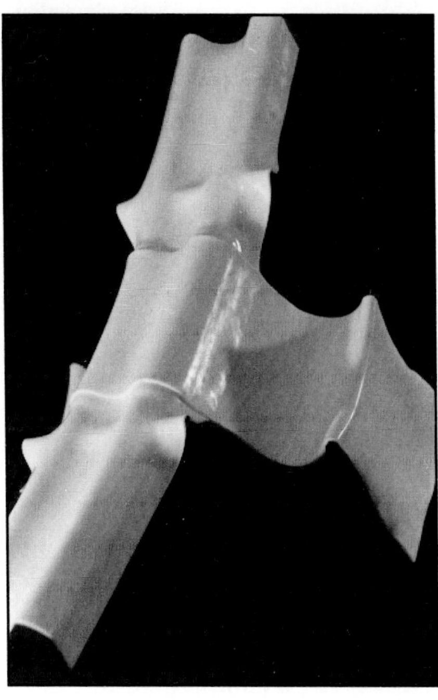

Glass sculptural form, 14" x 25", created by sagging glass over copper wire suspended from outside top edge of kiln.

SAGGING THROUGH STRETCHED WIRE

Stretching copper wire across a side-fire kiln, then placing glass over the wire and sagging the glass, can create an unlimited variety of forms. Functional bowl forms, vases and sculptural forms can be made with this process.

Heavy gauge copper ground cable can be obtained at most hardware stores. The copper wire should be coated with a heavy coating of shelf primer. Mix the shelf primer 1 part to 2 parts with water to make a heavy, creamy paste. After placing the wire in the kiln, heat it to 200°F, then paint one thick coat of primer over the wire. Let it dry completely before placing glass on top.

Wire can be attached to the kiln by placing it between the top of the kiln and the lid or by placing the wire between the rings of a multiple ring kiln. Stretching wires across a heavy metal frame that sits inside of the kiln or drilling holes through the side of the kiln is also a possibility.

The glass to be sagged can be multiple layers of any glass or pre-fused glass blanks. If some areas have more glass, the extra weight will cause the glass to sag faster in those areas. Forms made with this process can be cut apart and reassembled, adding infinite variety to sculptural forms.

Some wires oxidize, leaving a black residue on the glass. This can be removed with sandblasting. Wire can be wrapped with fiber paper, and held with staples.

Constructed, clear, sagged forms cast into Ultracal base.

Annealing wire sagged forms is very direct, since most glasses will anneal by just letting the kiln cool at its natural rate. The wire cools at a similar rate to the glass and is affected by the glass, since there is no other mold to cause uneven cooling. Annealing is not usually a problem, no matter how large the glass piece.

AN OVERVIEW

Glass tiles ready to be slumped are usually larger, thicker and often more uneven than during initial fusing and this glass is effected by the mold and the material it's made from, so more attention must be given to the even heating of the glass to avoid thermal shock. Understanding how glass heats, and the factors that affect its heating rate, can often be best understood by drawing a diagram of the glass on the mold in the kiln. This visual representation should include an indication of materials that could affect the thermal gradient within the glass. Such a diagram and observation of the glass during firing will prevent more potential problems than can be covered in any book. The following general notes should be considered for all slumping and sagging situations.

1. Thermal shock is cause by *uneven heating or cooling.*
2. Whenever possible, molds should be uniform in thickness.
3. Vent holes should be placed in the parts of the mold that will fill *last* - not always the lowest points within the mold cavity.
4. Shelf primer should be applied to all molds and allowed to dry.
5. Steep, vertical sides should be avoided when creating mold shapes, but can be achieved with multiple slumps.
6. Molds should be *level* before firing.
7. Molds should be slightly elevated from the kiln floor.
8. Slumping and sagging should be performed slowly, maximizing control over the movement of the glass.

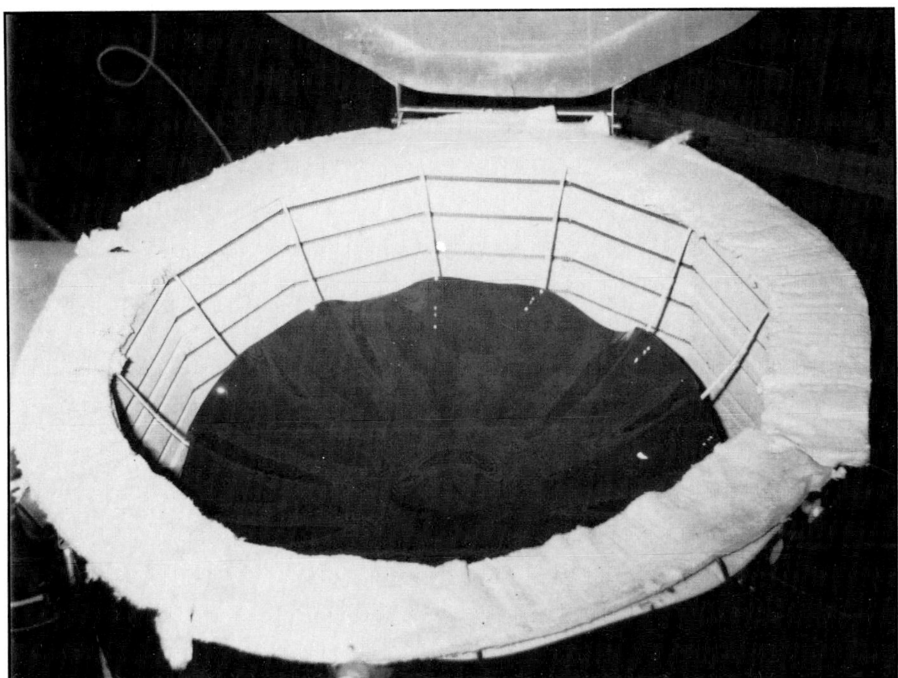

A Vitrolite glass circle, 24" wide, slumping through spaces between twelve copper wires, supported around the kiln top edge.

Beautiful lady selling musk melons from Vitrolite bowl.

CHAPTER EIGHT

Problem Solving

READING THE BREAKS

If I could control such things, in the best of all worlds glass fusing and annealing would work successfully for everyone with his first effort and every time thereafter. But since the glass fusing process has been reintroduced as a craft and an art form so recently, not enough practical knowledge has been compiled to assure successful pieces from every firing. Furthermore, the learning curve of most students of fusing requires the individual gathering of practical knowledge. That's the breaks!

Many general conclusions as to why glass breaks, and the relationship of the shape of the crack to its cause, have been compiled during the course of our classes at Camp Colton. Many students are ambitious and push to accomplish a body of work during the class, in addition to acquiring technical information. This rush to accomplish often leads to problems with the glass, but since we all keep good notes and graph all the firings, a body of practical knowledge about breaks has been developed. I believe that the information presented here is of use and generally accurate, but it is formulated by personal observation and not from scientific testing.

Spider web cracking, thermal shock cracks, stress-related cracks caused by poor annealing, and incompatibility cracks all look different. If the observation of these cracks can be understood (read), time and materials can be saved in correcting the cause.

Small, interconnecting cracks extending out from one point in the glass piece, but not causing it to fall apart, may be apparent after removing it from the kiln shelf. This is called spider web cracking and is usually attributed to glass sticking to the kiln shelf. No other physical evidence may be apparent on first observation. Shelf primer may or may not be stuck to the back side of the glass. Upon closer observation, there will usually be noticeable very small pieces of glass stuck to the kiln shelf at the point where the center of the spider web fracture interconnects. This kind of cracking may happen to a piece of glass that has been combed. If the glass rake used for combing is inserted into the surface of the glass too deeply the shelf primer is disturbed and the glass sticks to the shelf.

When large volumes of glass are melted flat, the movement of the glass flowing across the primer-coated shelf surface may cause primer to thin, allowing the glass to stick. Small scratches in the shelf primer, caused by moving glass across the shelf while arranging it, or simply inadequate application of shelf primer may cause this kind of cracking.

Another kind of spider web cracking is caused by crystal formation within the matrix of the glass. I have only observed this in red glasses made with cadmium and selenium. The interconnected cracks appear after the second or third firing of the same piece, never after the first firing. Therefore, I believe that the spider web cracking is caused by crystal growth or continued striking of the selenium. The only solution in this case is to avoid use of specific red glass that causes the problem.

Thermal shock cracks that happen during the initial heating usually start in the center of the bottom blank and break it into seven to ten pie-shaped pieces. When a large bottom blank breaks, it often has enough force to shoot pie-shaped pieces off of the edge of the kiln shelf. Thermal shock is not always caused by fast heating, and is sometimes the result of uneven heating. A thermal gradient will exist across a piece of glass if one part of the blank is exposed to the radiant heat of the element and another area is insulated with a stack of glass placed on top of the blank. This potential thermal shock situation is most often corrected by changing stacking techniques. Cutting large blanks into three or four pieces, along design lines, making the bottom blank into smaller pieces will help avoid thermal cracking.

Thermal shock most often occurs as the pyrometer reaches 300-400°F. The heating rate of some kilns when on the lowest setting can be too fast for pieces constructed with bottom blanks more than 16 inches across. There are two types of infinite switches: those that give 15% current on low and those that give 27% current on low. Those kilns that have higher current switches should have the infinite switches replaced, or the kiln can be watched closely and the switch turned on and off every five minutes. The lid can be cracked on a top firing kiln for some adjustment, but I do not suggest cracking the door open on a front leading kiln, since this situation will definitely cause a thermal gradient.

I suggest to all of my students that they check the progress of their firing at 400°F by peeking, either lifting the lid or opening the door, to be certain that the glass has not thermal shocked. If the glass has thermal shocked, the kiln can be cooled and the glass arranged back together. At this point, little is lost, but if fired past the laminating temperature of the glass, the piece cannot be moved back together.

Cracks caused by thermal shock after the glass has been fully fused usually form one of two distinctive patterns. An annealed piece of glass breaks in a straight line or a slightly curved line across the *middle* of the piece. Glass that has been poorly annealed breaks in an S curve or into three pieces, with all the breaks showing a distinctive curved pattern. A piece of glass breaks in half because this relieves most of the stress. An S line break is any break that curves within the last one inch before exiting the glass form. If this becomes a reoccurring problem, the annealing temperature should be raised and a longer time spent in the annealing zone.

Breaks due to incompatibility look different than any other breaks. When incompatible glass is present, the break will follow one or two edges of the shape of the incompatible glass. It is not unusual for the glass to break into three or four pieces, with other fractures starting into the glass piece from the incompatible glass, but not causing a complete separation.

Hopefully, most of these common breaks will not have to be observed often. But if they have been a problem, perhaps reading the breaks will guide you to a quick and successful solution.

MAGAZINES

American Craft, American Craft Council, 40 W. 53rd St., New York, NY 10019.

Crafts Magazine, 8 waterloo Pl., London, Great Britain, SW 1Y4AT.

Glass Art Magazine, 1008 Depot Hill Office Park, Broomfield, CO 80020.

Industrial Heating, P. O. Box 1256, Troy, MI 48099.

Neues Glas, Ver laganstalt Handwerk GnBH, Postfach 8 120, D 4000, Dusseldorf, West Germany.

New Work, The Glass Workshop, 142 Mulberry St., New York, NY 10013.

Professional Stained Glass, Tonetta Lake Road, P.O. Box 69, Brewster, NY 10509

Stained Glass Quarterly, 4050 Broadway, Kansas City, MO 64111.

U.S. Glass, 560 Oakwood, Suite 202, Lake Forest, IL 60045.

Myles smiles as he shows off the Glass Glow 300 D. This kiln is larger than it looks; Myles is big.

Glass Glow 560 kiln with 20" x 40" usable space.

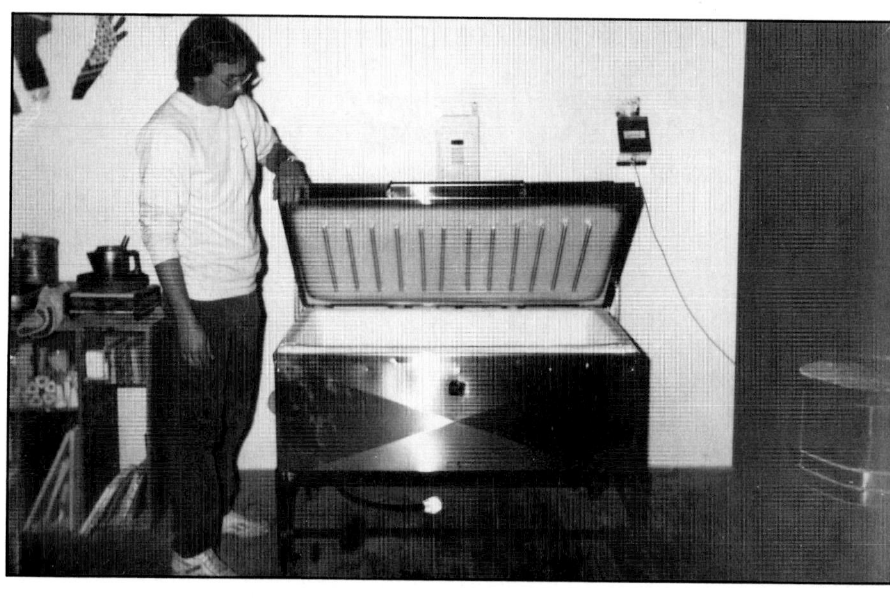

CHAPTER NINE

Fusing Equipment

KILNS

A glass fusing kiln must have the capability to heat glass evenly to at least 1600°F, and provide a means of monitoring, controlling, and observing the various stages of firing. A kiln of any size, used or new, that fits these criteria can be used to fuse and anneal glass successfully, as long as the user understands the potential of the kiln and designs projects within that scope.

Presently, there are at least eight manufacturers making kilns especially for glass fusing. Among the offerings of these companies there exists a wide variety of formats for fusers, with and without controllers, and a wide range of prices.

At Camp Colton we use glass fusing kilns by three of these companies, as well as two varieties of studio-built kilns that provide a larger firing space than do those commercially available. We use the Glass Glow 300 D and 560, the Paragon 22 A, and the Skutt Octagon 16 and 1227. These represent, in total, a variety of formats in regard to size, element placement, and controlling capabilities. They were chosen to satisfy the needs of a diversified, changing group of students.

Many students ask me on the first day of class what fusing kiln is "the best". I have the impression that they want to learn to use that particular kiln, assuming they will buy that kiln model, and not need to learn to fire any other. Of course, there is no "best" kiln. There are many things to consider in choosing a kiln, the most important of which is the work habits and goals of the intended user.

After a person has decided on a glass working format or designed a series of glass pieces that will satisfy his goals, it becomes a lot easier to make an informed decision. Lacking this opportunity, the following things should be considered: price, firing capacity, firing controls, element placement, and safety features.

Is it done yet?

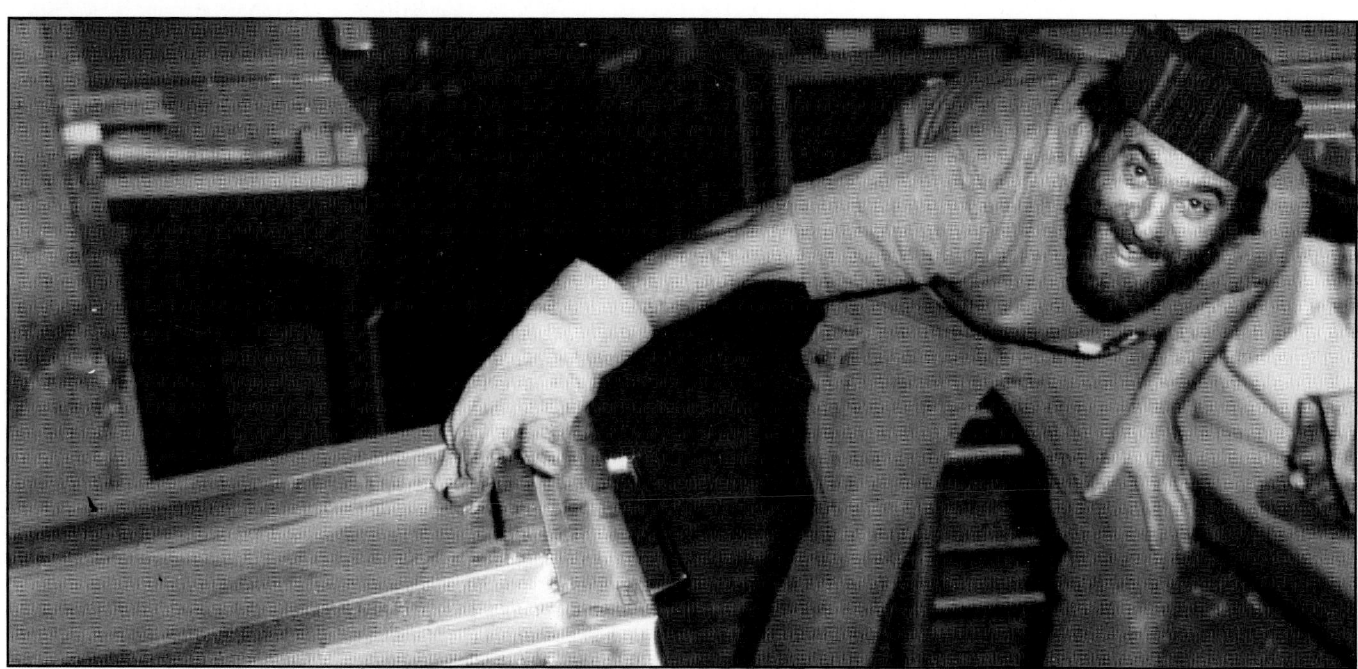

Looking into a front-loading Paragon 22A. It is easy to observe the slumping process with a front-loading kiln.

The price of glass fusing kilns is the biggest variable, and not always related to the size or amount of work that can be produced in a particular kiln. A used ceramic kiln, 16" to 27" wide and up to 27" deep can be purchased for $300 to $600 through classified ads in metropolitan areas. Some ceramic supply houses resell their customers used kilns at reasonable prices. New ceramic kilns and fusing kilns range in price from $350 to $2000, with a reasonably large choice available in the $800 to $1200 range.

Fusing kilns with special features, such as top and bottom elements, or programmable controllers, are available, on request, from many of the companies making glass fusing kilns. In other words, kilns can be commercially made to order.

Designing and building your own kiln is a potential solution to both cost and configuration. But my advice to students is to avoid building if they can buy a commercially built kiln that meets the requirements, unless kiln construction holds a special appeal for them. The time it takes to learn how to build a kiln and then gather the materials and construct the unit is enough that it becomes a reverse economy, if you'd really rather be fusing. However, if you need a kiln two feet wide and ten feet long, building it yourself may be the best solution.

Electric kilns used for fusing have heating elements either on the inside top of the kiln or around the inside walls of the kiln. Top-fired kilns radiate heat downward from the elements over the entire surface of the glass on the shelf. All of the glass exposed to the elements receives the same quantity of heat at the same time, so control of the thermal gradient across a large piece of glass is easier and the glass can usually be fired faster during initial heat up without thermal shocking the glass.

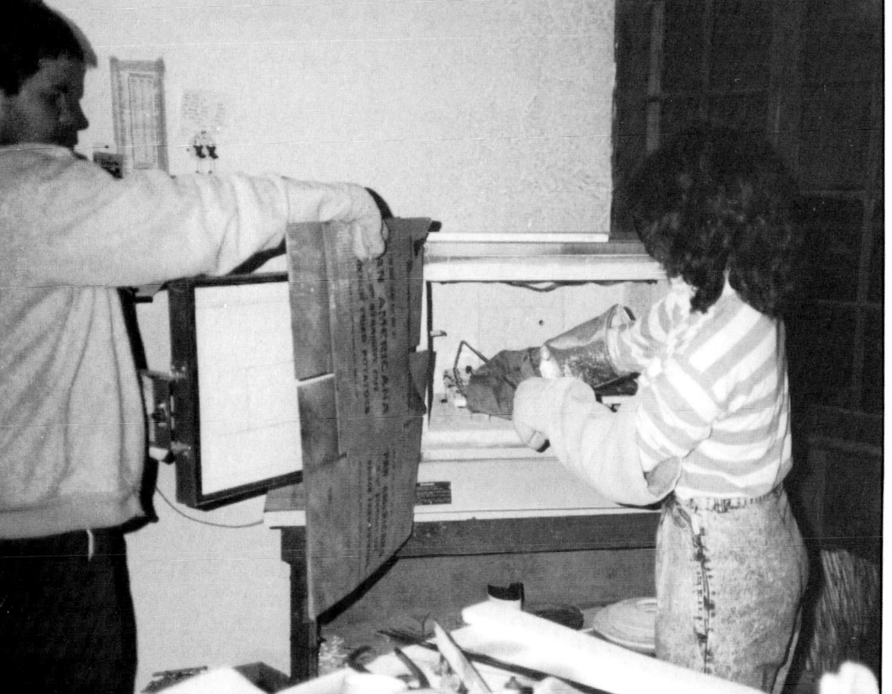

Looking into a Paragon 22A. Notice how the door is designed to inset into kiln chamber to reduce heat loss.

Opening the front-loading Paragon while hot to manipulate the molten glass. A tin sheet is held in front of the door to minimize radiated heat.

Side-fired kilns have the advantage of being capable of firing several shelves at one time, an impossibility with a top-fired kiln. The proper spacing between shelves must be found by experimentation, in order to achieve the same "heat soak" on each shelf. The glass on the outer perimeter of a side-fired kiln receives heat before the glass in the center of the shelf only when the shelf is elevated above the first row of side elements. When only one shelf at a time is fired in a side-fired kiln, and that shelf is only 1 1/2" off of the bottom of the kiln, it fires just like a top-fired kiln, because all of the elements and most of the heat are above the kiln shelf. When two or more shelves are stacked in a side-fired kiln, the glass on the outer perimeter of the shelf receives heat sooner than does the glass in the center of the shelf. This causes the temperature of the glass in the center to lag behind the temperature of the glass around the outside, during initial heat. If this thermal gradient is too great, the unequal expansion will cause the glass to break. Because of this, firings of more than one shelf in a side-fired kiln must be fired slower than would be the case in a top-fired kiln.

Fusing kilns are insulated with either insulating fire brick (soft brick) or ceramic fiber insulation. The soft brick will soak up more heat than the fiber in the heat up cycle, but upon cooling will give some of this heat back to the kiln. Therefore, the natural cooling rate of a soft brick kiln is often slow enough that the kiln will not have to be fired down, except during the annealing cycle. In contrast, fiber-insulated kilns require adding heat during the annealing cycle and beyond it in order to avoid thermal shock. The manufacturers of these two types of kilns have designed their controllers so that both types have good cooling curves.

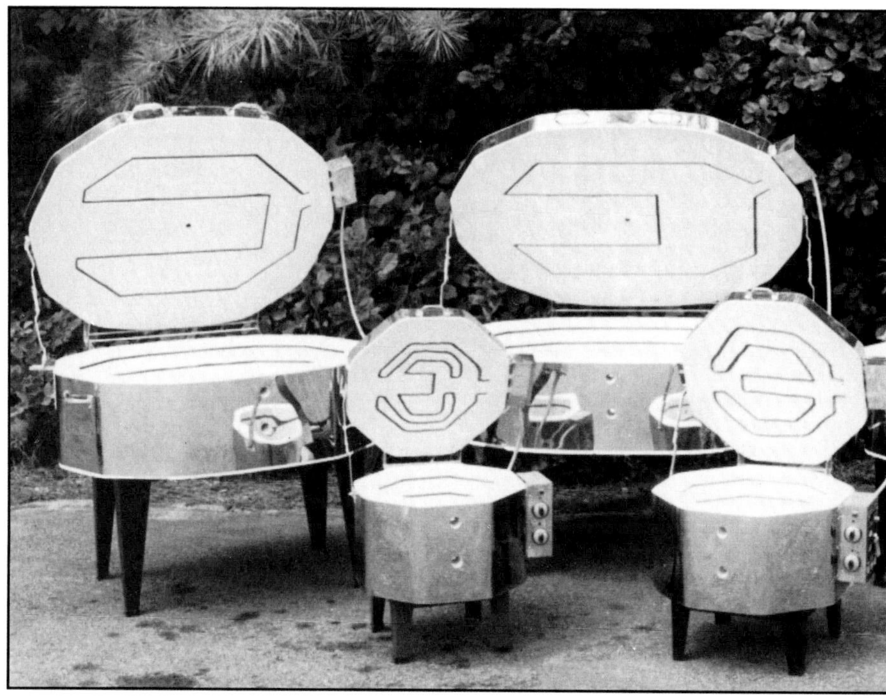

Olympic kilns designed with both top and side heating elements.

There are two possible door locations for kilns: the door, or lid, on the top (called top loader) or the door in front (called front loader). Top loading kilns have the advantage of allowing easy access to the entire top surface of the fusing project. Front loading ovens allow less access to the top, but provide a full view of the side, an advantage when slumping or sagging. In large top loading kilns the weight of the door or lid can be a burden, and building a project on the shelf in the kiln may require a lot of bending over. Neither of these physical realities is a problem with a front loader, but loading a full kiln shelf into a front loader takes plenty of physical strength, and if pieces of glass have shifted while the shelf was being carried and loaded, they will be difficult to see.

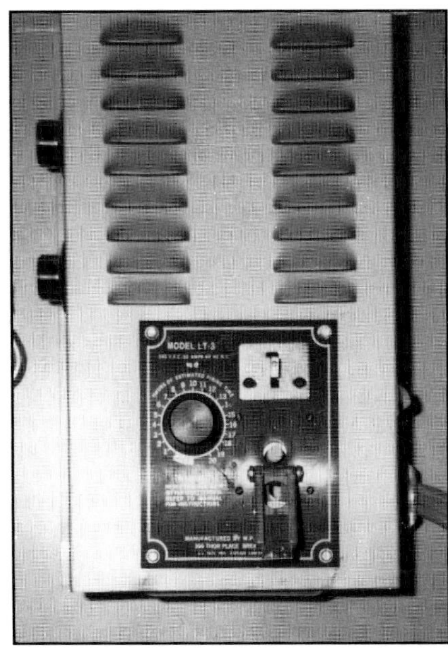

Double security, a time limit switch and a kiln sitter.

A real pair! Two Skutt Octogan 16's, one with a 4-1/2" blank expansion ring. I've used these two kilns for 7 years.

The controls available on fusing kilns today are more sophisticated than when fusing kilns were first on the market. Any combination of timers, kiln sitters, infinite switches, set-point controllers, or programmable controllers may be ordered to fit a particular fusing kiln. The infinite switch is standard on all kilns made for fusing. It controls the percentage of "on" time by cycling the power on for a number of seconds and then off for a number of seconds. This switch has from six to ten positions that truly give infinite control.

This simple, standard switch, in conjunction with a timer offers safety and ease of control through a long annealing cycle, but requires more diligence and time in learning about the firing characteristics of a particular kiln. A solid state programmable controller fires as accurately as the program punched into it. The choice of what control device to use is a matter of preference and ability to justify expense. Given the choice, most of my advanced students would choose the programmable controller.

Boyce manipulates the glass in a 40" x 40" user-built kiln. The kiln is suspended from the ceiling rafters. The shelf and floor rolls out from under the kiln for easy access.

Side view of 40" x 40" fusing kiln, showing electric elements under shelf, a necessity when fusing and annealing large glass slabs.

CONTROLLERS

Present technology of solid state memory, which can be programmed simply by punching in the desired time and temperature cycle on a small keyboard, is becoming less expensive every year. In the past two years, I have noticed the price of a fully programmable fusing controller decrease by $400.00. Indications I receive from kiln manufacturers are that controllers will do more and cost less in the near future.

I believe the advantages of a controller far outweigh the expense, once you have a full understanding of all the processes that you will program into the controller. In other words, don't get a controller until you know all of the eccentricities of the fusing kiln in use, and how it operates manually.

There are three types of automatic controllers available: the set-point controller, which allows you to dial a control knob to the desired temperature, which will be reached and held until the setting is adjusted; the cam controller, which allows the complete firing schedule to be mapped out on a plastic cam, allowing the firing to mechanically follow the plan on the cam; and the programmable controller, which contains a small computer.

The set-point controller is the least expensive and the programmable controller the most expensive. Of the five controllers that I have tested to date, the programmable controller from Advanced Technical Services, Inc. is the easiest to program and seems to accept the largest range of programs.

Paragon controller.

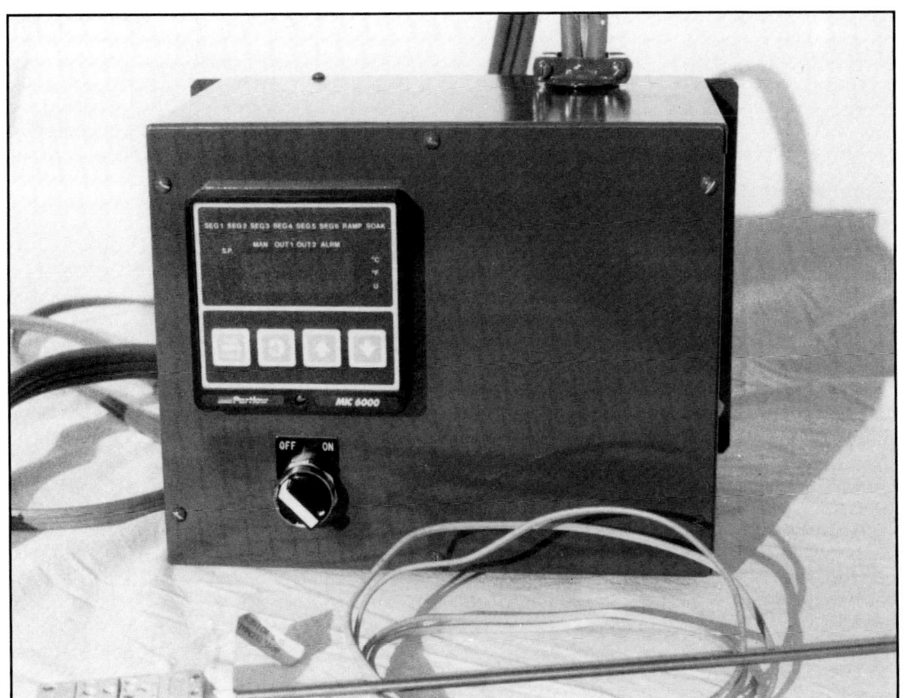

KilnWizard controller.

DIAMOND TECHNOLOGY

Many advancements have been made in the past ten years in the technology of attaching diamonds to various metals for grinding and sawing applications. For the glass artist, the important advancement has been the availability of diamond blade saws and diamond grinders that are affordable and functional for the small glass working studio. It is hard to resist owning diamond cutting and grinding equipment in a personal studio, because, for a modest investment, one can add much dimension to finished work.

Diamond grinding and polishing of fused glass can greatly enhance the appearance of a finished piece. Previously fused pieces can be sawn, shifted, and re-fused into a new design. Diamond band saws allow the cutting of tight inside curves and intricate shapes.

I believe that the equipment presented for use to my students should be commercially available at an affordable price. In the not- too-distant past the only diamond equipment available was built for industry, and was too expensive to purchase for the individual studio. It many be exciting for a student to use a $2600 diamond lap grinding wheel, but it does not function as an educational experience, if it will not be available to that student in the future. At Camp Colton we have been able to put some of the affordable diamond technology to a good test. Class after class of students uses the same saws and grinders for a variety of applications. Diamond tools that hold up in such a situation can be expected to last a long time in a personal studio with only one or two operators.

We have tried a number of diamond saws, grinders, and polishing equipment in our classes, and the general consensus is that, for diversity of function and value for cost, the Sculpture Router, by Gemstone, is the best first piece of add-on equipment for a fusing studio. Its unique three-inch diamond cutting wheel is used for cutting inside radii, as well as rough edge-grinding of fused glass up to 3/16" thick. One grinding wheel often lasts through 40 or 50 students before it must be replaced. The eight-inch Dynamo Trim Saw, by Gemstone, also stands up to continued student use. Its internal water pump recirculates water and coolant to both sides of the diamond blade. This cooling system makes blades last a long time. The fact that it is a chop saw with a top-mounted motor and blade does limit the length of a cut to approximately ten inches. These two pieces of equipment are readily available and can form the backbone of diamond tools useful in an individual studio.

Flat surfaces and edges can be ground and polished with diamond sandpaper attached with glue or velcro to an orbital sander. Diamond pads for disc grinders and rubber-backed hand sand pads are also available. Diamond drills and all the necessary adaptors to modify a standard drill press for water cooled drilling are presently available at affordable prices.

The Gemstone Sculpture Router.

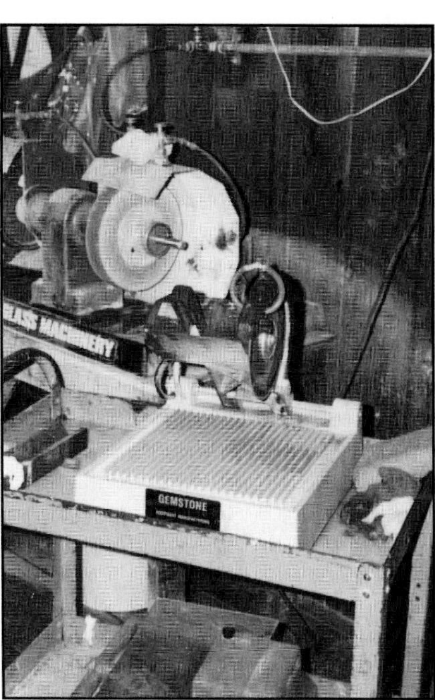

The 8" Dynamo Trim Saw.

The best way to find out about craft equipment that uses diamond technology is to write to the companies. It is not my intent in this chapter to act as an advertisement for specific pieces of equipment, but to increase your awareness of the *kind* of things that may be found, as well as to pass on some of the positive experiences we've gained through testing.

Before making an investment in a piece of equipment, evaluate what function it will be expected to serve in *your* studio, and be certain, through the manufacturer or other recommendations, that it will perform that function. Perhaps a comparable piece of equipment will perform as well and be more versatile. Articles and reviews of most items presented here are published by *Professional Stained Glass* and *Glass Art Magazine*. Trade shows and other glass artists are good sources of information about any glass working equipment.

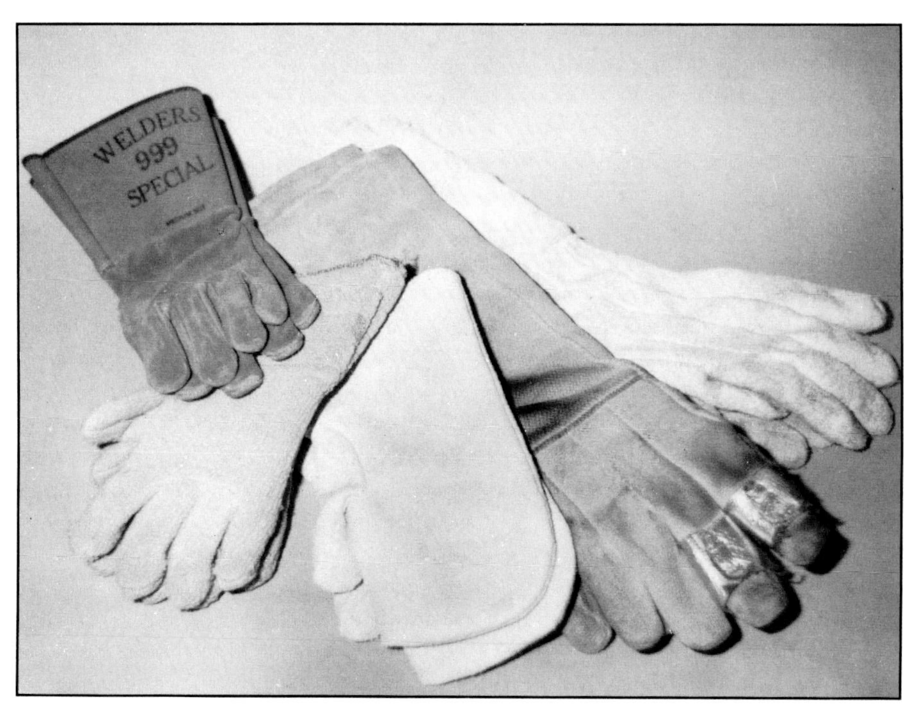
WELDERS
999
SPECIAL

CHAPTER TEN

SAFETY

The intent of this section is to encourage awareness of potential hazards in the studio environment. As we become more knowledgeable about our environment, it becomes obvious that, as glass artists, we are surrounded by a variety of potentially hazardous materials and situations.

Common sense can play an important role in reducing or limiting dangerous exposure, and in maintaining a healthy studio environment. For example, materials that irritate the skin will invariably irritate the eyes and the respiratory tract. Materials such as paints and enamels, which contain lead and other metals, and which should not be inhaled in powdered form, may give off fumes when fired. The judicious use of gloves, safety glasses, and/or a respirator equipped with filters appropriate to the hazards involved will help minimize undesirable exposure. Confining use of hazardous materials to a particular area in the studio, good studio housekeeping habits, and the addition of exhaust ventilation localized to specific areas of the studio are other simple ways to minimize hazards.

PRODUCTS WHICH REQUIRE ATTENTION

SHELF PRIMER/KILN WASH contains silica (quartz) and is, therefore, hazardous to breathe in its dry form. Use localized ventilation or, better yet, work outdoors, when sanding shelf primer off of kiln shelves. Avoid inhaling the dust, as excessive exposure may cause silicosis. A respirator fitted with a filter approved for eliminating particulates should be worn when dust is created in an unventilated area.

CALCIUM CARBONATE is considered harmless but, in its raw form, may contain other minerals. Avoid inhaling dusts, since any dust may cause eye, nose and throat irritation.

SQUEEGEE OIL is a liquid whose combustible byproducts are toxic. When squeegee oil is fired, kiln ventilation is crucial, to avoid iritation to eyes and lungs. It is important to wash skin thoroughly after contact with the liquid oil.

OVERGLAZES usually contain material from the lead silicate family. Take care when using any product containing lead. Avoid breathing the dust or mist, and use localized exhaust ventilation. Do not smoke, eat, or drink while working with these materials; wash skin thoroughly after contact with overglazes.

FIBER MOLD HARDENER may contain ethylene glycol, considered highly toxic. Avoid inhalation, contact with the skin, and any availability to children who could accidentally ingest this material. Venting the kiln of fumes when firing, and wearing rubber gloves when working with this material will reduce exposure.

FIBER PRODUCTS contain aluminosilicate and may be irritating to the skin, eyes, and respiratory system, as well as being a possible cancer hazard. A dusty form of the fibers is released when the material is handled to cut or tear. In addition, all fiber materials leave a white, powdery residue on the glass and the kiln shelf when fired that, when disturbed, may release potentially hazardous dust into the air. A respirator equipped with filters to remove particulates should be worn when handling fired fiber; clean glass under water to reduce dust.

Opposite page: Safety is very important but I'd rather be dead than look like these nerds.

ENAMELS AND PAINTS contain lead and other toxic metals. Localized ventilation and/or the use of an approved respirator should be employed, whenever working with these materials in either dry or spray form. Tools and the work area should be kept clean and gloves should be worn, if you have cuts, burns, or other skin problems. Never eat or smoke while working with these materials.

Firing these materials can cause metals and opacifiers to fume; kilns should be properly vented to prevent contamination of the work area.

FRITS are usually of large enough grain size that they are not ordinarily inhaled. However, since there may be "fines" present, small enough to be inhaled and cause lung damage, use of a respirator is recommended when handling glass frit.

CASTABLE MOLD MATERIALS including plasters, investments, refractories, sand, and clay in the dry form should be considered hazardous, since most contain silica and may cause serious lung damage. Avoid creating a dusty atmosphere, wear a respirator, and work in a well-ventilated area. Localized exhaust is recommended.

USE OF STUDIO EQUIPMENT

KILNS-When kiln firing we not only employ volatile substances, in materials other than glass, that can be hazardous, but the heating of these substances produces a variety of gases and vapors. These include organic combustion products from paints and oils, as well as fumes from lead and other metals, fumes from mold hardener, and particulates from fiber products.

To help reduce exposure, it is advisable to install a ventilation system for the kiln. This can be a commercial or custom-built hood or a venting system designed to attach to, and ventilate, a kiln. Several of these are on the market and are readily adaptable to most kilns.

Protective clothing should be worn when opening a hot kiln. Electric shock will be prevented by turning the kiln off before reaching inside to comb or manipulate glass.

FURNACES/GLORYHOLES-It is important to make reference to local fire regulations and other codes that will affect the placement and use of furnaces and glory holes and the placement of propane tanks.

Bottled gases should be treated with respect; tanks should be secured and fittings well maintained. Where furnaces are fueled with natural gas piped to the burner, a periodic check of the fittings and joints with soapy water will reveal any leaks. Keeping gas plumbing in good repair will prevent explosions from escaped gas.

Safety glasses should be worn to protect your eyes, not only from flying glass shards, but from infrared light produced by the intense heat source. Prolonged exposure can cause cataracts.

Don't smoke and wear your glasses upside down. Mike Dupille, Ruth Brockman, Dan Ott and Boyce are 1) sometimes confused about safety, 2) will die of cancer and/or 3) are looking for trouble.

Non-asbestos gloves, such as those made of Kevlar or Zetex, and clothing made of natural fibers can protect hands and arms during hot glass sessions.

An indoor glass furnace should be equipped with a localized ventilation system, to insure that the studio is not contaminated with fumes from the glass melt.

GRINDING AND POLISHING-Glass dust from "cold working" is hazardous. During wet grinding, glass dust accumulates as a paste and, when dry, becomes a hazardous powder. Equipment, clothing and work areas should be kept clean and a respirator worn, when necessary.

Common sense care should be taken around all "cold working" machinery, as with all power tools. Guards should be installed on grinding wheels and shafts that may catch hair or clothing. Safety glasses should be worn to protect the eyes from flying shards of glass.

SAFETY EQUIPMENT

RESPIRATORS can be very effective in situations where specific localized exhaust ventilation is not possible. Respirators such as we use in our studio consist of a silicone mask worn over the nose and mouth, with a cylindrically-shaped, replaceable filter cartridge on either side of the face. Filters are designed for specific types of hazardous exposure.

It should be noted, however, that respirators do have drawbacks. In glass work we are exposed to particulates, fumes or both. Problems arise because fumes easily penetrate dust filters and dust quickly clogs fume filters. It is important to use the proper filter for the exposure, the best choice being a combination, a fume filter with a dust pre-filter. Respirators are not 100% effective and are not a substitute for good ventilation.

Respirators come in many sizes and shapes. Three companies that manufacture a variety of approved devices are:

Willson Co.
Division of WGM Safety Corp.
2nd and Washington Streets
Reading, PA

Survivair Division
U.S.D. Corp.
Santa Ana, CA

American Optical Corporation
P.O. Box 1
Southbridge, MA 01550

Check local safety supply outlets for additional information, or call manufacturers for names of distributors.

SAFETY GLASSES-Infrared wavelengths of light are produced by intense heat sources such as kilns, furnaces, and glory holes. Prolonged exposure to infrared light can cause cataracts. Glassworkers should always use protective glasses, when looking at infrared sources.

Calobar lenses block infrared, while transmitting visible wavelengths. This protects you from overexposure and still allows viewing of your work.

American Optical supplies data on three shades of Calobar lenses:

medium transmits:	52% visible light
	9% infrared
dark transmits:	33% visible light
	4.5% infrared
x-dark transmits:	17% visible light
	1% infrared

Didymium lenses should not be substituted for calobar lenses, as they filter only 20% of the infrared, not adequate protection. American Optical manufactures a variety of Calobar lenses which are available through local distributors.

GLOVES-Heat from equipment such as kilns, furnaces and glory holes, as well as from the glass itself can cause serious burns. Heat resistant gloves are a necessity for hot glass work and all activities involving a hot kiln. Gloves such as Zetex and Kevlar are available through most fusing and ceramic suppliers, and from:

Tempo Glove Mfg., Inc.
3820 W. Wisconsin Ave.
Milwaukee, Wisconsin 53208

A.R.T.CO
348 N. 15th St.
San Jose, CA 95112

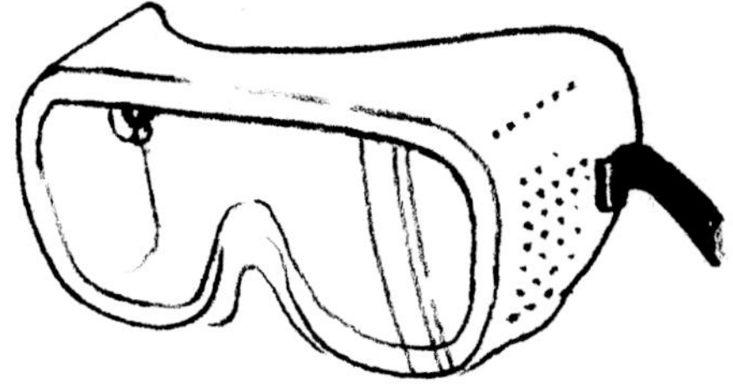

HOODS AND VENTS- Arranging good ventilation throughout the studio and localized ventilation, specific to problem areas, is the best way to avoid exposure to hazardous substances.

Use of a specially designed kiln ventilator is one way to achieve specific ventilation for fumes created in a hot kiln. There are several systems available commercially that can be added to most kilns:

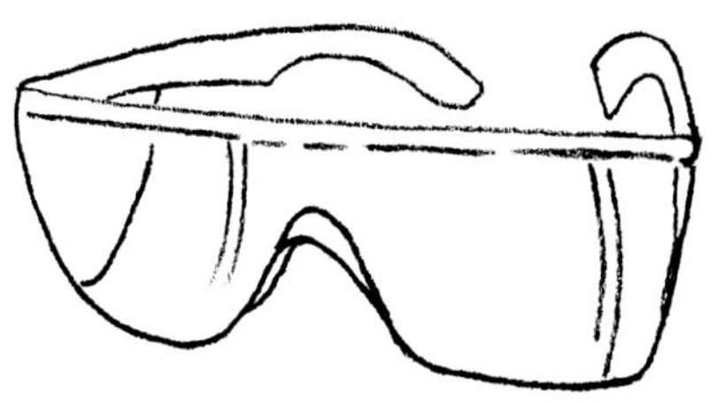

"Envirovent"
Skutt Ceramic Products
Portland, Oregon

"Direct Fume Vent System"
Bailey Ceramic Supply
Kingston , New York

"Vent-A-Kiln System"
Vent-A-Kiln Corp."
Buffalo, New York

AN OVERVIEW

Awareness of such things as fumes, dust, and skin irritations and response to them with intelligent precautions will go a long way in preserving your health. *Pay close attention to warning labels and product safety information!* Some specific solutions for securing a healthy work environment are:

1. Use a respirator with filters approved for dust and fumes, when the situation suggests this precaution.
2. Install localized exhaust ventilation for specific problem areas.
3. Wear protective clothing (gloves, etc.) when working with irritants and other hazardous materials.
4. Keep the work area clean, vacuuming and mopping, as opposed to sweeping.
5. Lay out the studio so that problem areas are somewhat isolated and do not contaminate the entire studio. These areas should be easily ventilated.

MANUFACTURERS

CRUCIBLES

Cercon Ceramic Consultants, Inc.
P.O. Box 116
Hermann, MO 65041

Laclede-Christy Co.
P.O. Box 550
Owensville, MO 65066

ENAMELS, PAINTS AND LUSTRES

Drakenfeld Colors
P.O. Box 519
Washington, PA 15301

Englehard Corp.
Hanovia Hobby Products
Menlo Park, CN28
Edison, NJ 08818

L.Reusche & Co.
2-6 Lister Ave.
Newark, NJ 07105

Thompson Enamel
650 Colfax Ave.
Newport, KY 41072

FIBER PRODUCTS

Babcock & Wilcox Co.
Insulating Products Division
Augusta, GA 30903

Carborundum Resistant Materials Co.
Insulation Division
P.O. Box 808
Niagra Falls, NY 14302

C-E Refractories
P.O. Box 828
Valley Forge, PA 19482

Johns Manville Insulation
Drawer 17L
Denver, CO 80217

WRP
P.O. Box 2134
Elgin, IL 60120

Zircar
110 N. Main St.
Florida, NY 10921

GLASS CULLET, FRIT, FUSIBLE SHEET AND ROD

Bullseye Glass Co.
3722 S.E. 21st Ave.
Portland, OR 97202
(fusible sheet)

Corning Glass Works
Corning, NY 14830
(rods, tubing)

Glass Hues, Inc.
5650 Jason Lee Place
Sarasota, FL 33583
813-923-3334
(fusible sheet, frit, stringer)

Louie Glass Co., Inc.
Weston, WV 26452
(cullet)

Northstar Glassworks
9060 S.W. Sunstead Lane
Portland, OR 97225
(colored borosilicate)

Scott America/Desag
3 Odell Plaza
Yonkers, NY 10701
(fusible sheet)

Spruce Pine Batch Co.
Highway 19E
Spruce Pine, NC 28777
(glass batch)

Vitreous Group/Camp Colton
Colton, OR 97017
(glass stringer)

GLASS BLOWING TOOLS AND EQUIPMENT

A.R.T.CO
348 N. 15th St.
San Jose, CA 95112

Steinert Pipes and Rods
1000 Mogadore Rd.
Kent, Ohio 44240

GRINDING, POLISHING, AND SAWING EQUIPMENT

Amazing Glazing
2929 E. Coon Lake Rd.
Howell, MI 48843

Covington Engineering Corp.
715 West Colton Ave.
Redlands, CA 92373

C.R. Laurence Co., Inc.
2503 E. Vernon
Los Angeles, CA 90058

Crystalite Corporation
13449 Beach Ave.
Marina Del Rey, CA 90292

Gemstone Equipment Mfg. Co.
750 Easy St.
Simi Valley, CA 93065

Glastar Corp.
19515 Business Center Drive
Northridge, CA 91324

Gryphon Corp.
101 E. Santa Anita Ave.
Burbank, CA 91502

Inland Craft Product Co.
32046 Edward
Madison Heights, MI 32046

MWP Associates
Box 99775
San Francisco, CA 94107

KILNS

Aerospex Company
1433 Roosevelt Ave.
National City, CA 90205

Denver Glass Machinery
3065 Umatilla St.
Englewood, CO 80110

Glass Glow
4556 Auburn Blvd.
Sacramento, CA 95841

Jen Ken Kilns
4569 Samuel St.
Sarasota, FL 95841

Olympic Kilns
6301 Button Gwinnett Dr.
Atlanta, DA 30340

Paragon Industries
Box 850808
Mesquite, TX 75185

Seattle Pottery Supply
35 South Hanford
Seattle,WA 98134

Skutt Ceramics
2618 S.E. Steele St.
Portland, OR 97202

KILN CONTROLLERS

Advanced Technical Services,Inc
21045 Des Moines Memorial Dr.
Des Moines, WA 98198

Digitry Company
33 Ship Ave.
Medford, MA 02155

Edward Orton Jr. Ceramic Foundation
P.O. Box 460
Westerville, OH 43081

Kilntrol
8546 Madison Ave.
Fair Oaks, CA 95628

Paragon Industries
P.O. Box 850808
Mesquite, TX 75185

Seattle Pottery Supply
35 South Hanford
Seattle, WA 98134

MOLD MATERIALS

Perma Flex Mold Co.
1919 E. Livingston St.
Columbus, OH 43209

Ransom & Randolf
2337 Yates Ave.
Los Angeles, CA 90040

United States Gypsum
Tooling & Casting Division
101 S. Wacker Dr.
Chicago, IL 60606

RIGIDIZER

Carborundum Resistant Materials Co.
Insulation Division
P.O. Box 808
Niagra Falls, NY 14302

Zircar
110 N. Main St.
Florida, NY 10921

NEW RESOURCES

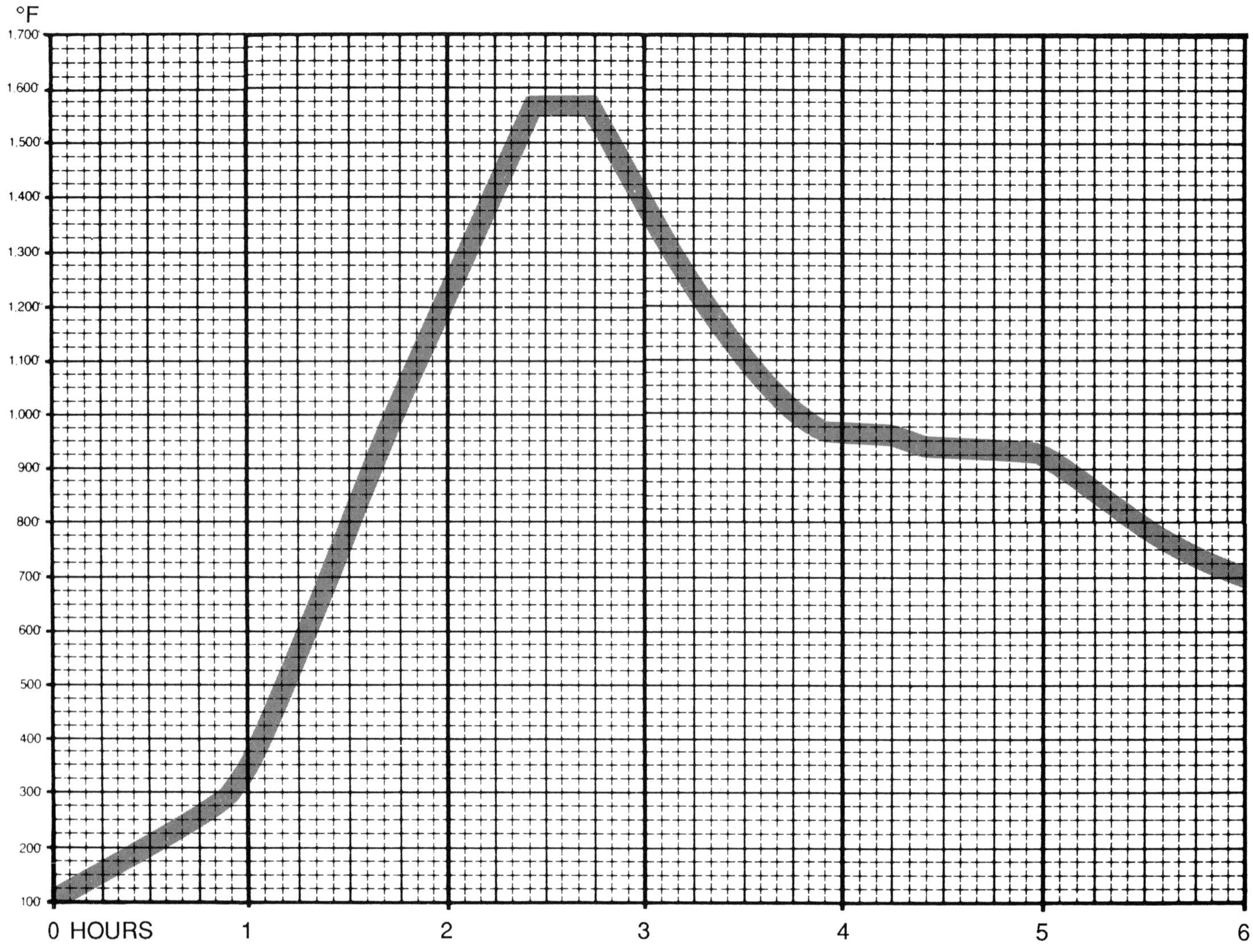

Temperature rise and annealing curve for 3/8" of glass.

FIRING AND ANNEALING

On these pages are graphs of the most commonly used firing and annealing procedures used in my classes. The first graph on pages 116 and 117 shows the initial heat cycle, the fuse soak, and the annealing schedule for fused work 1/4" to 3/8" thick and up to 12" across. When annealing glass pieces larger than 12 inches, I suggest adding ten minutes to the annealing time for each inch across over 12".

Temperatures shown on all graphs are pyrometer readings, not glass temperatures. The fact that the glass is cooler than the temperature reading on the pyrometer at the initial heat and hotter than the pyrometer indicates during cooling has been taken into consideration. The graphs are for 90 coefficient of expansion glasses.

The graph on page 118 shows annealing glass one-half inch thick and up to 12" across. Annealing time should be extended five minutes in each of the three annealing steps for each inch more than twelve inches across.

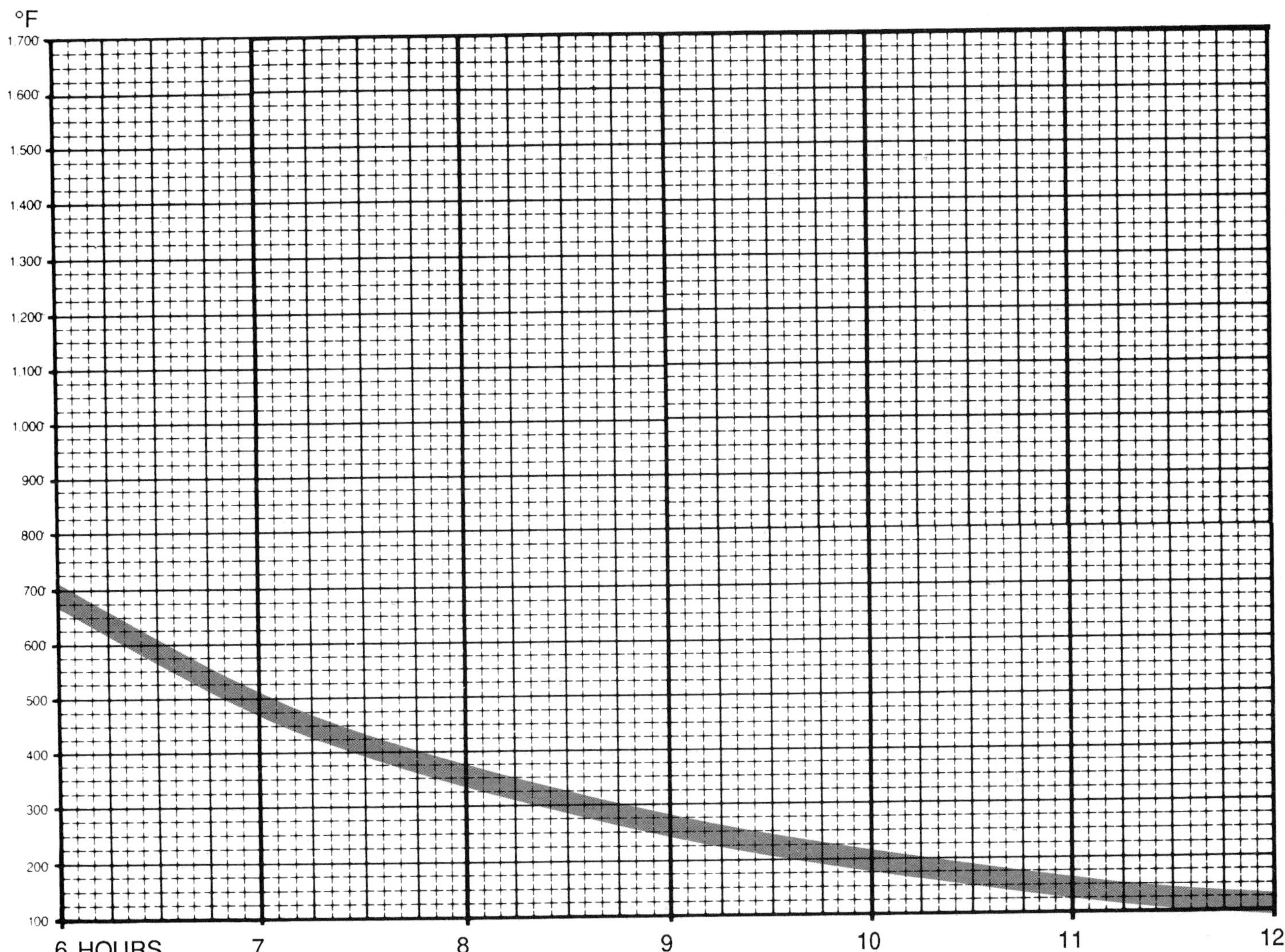

The graph on page 119 shows how to heat treat a piece of cast or fused glass up to two inches thick. This fast procedure works very well *if the object is fairly symmetrical, and does not change radically in thickness across the glass piece.* For example, a face or mask with a thickness of one-half inch at the edges, one inch at the cheeks, and two inches at the nose is commonly annealed in our classes using this schedule.

On pages 120 and 121 is a graph of the annealing time for a one inch glass slab, as suggested by Daniel Schwoerer in his technical paper at the end of this section.

When taking pieces of glass through the firing (heating) and annealing (cooling) stages there are three factors that should be kept in mind: the thickness of the piece or pieces of glass, the coefficient of expansion of the glass, and the size or volume of the finished object.

The initial heating stage consists of heating the glass from room temperature to above the strain point, about 850°F. During initial heating the outside of a piece of glass heats first and, as the molecules heat, they expand causing compression of the glass surface. If heating is not too rapid, the compression is balanced by tension in the middle of the glass piece. But if the thermal gradient is too large, the glass will break due to thermal shock.

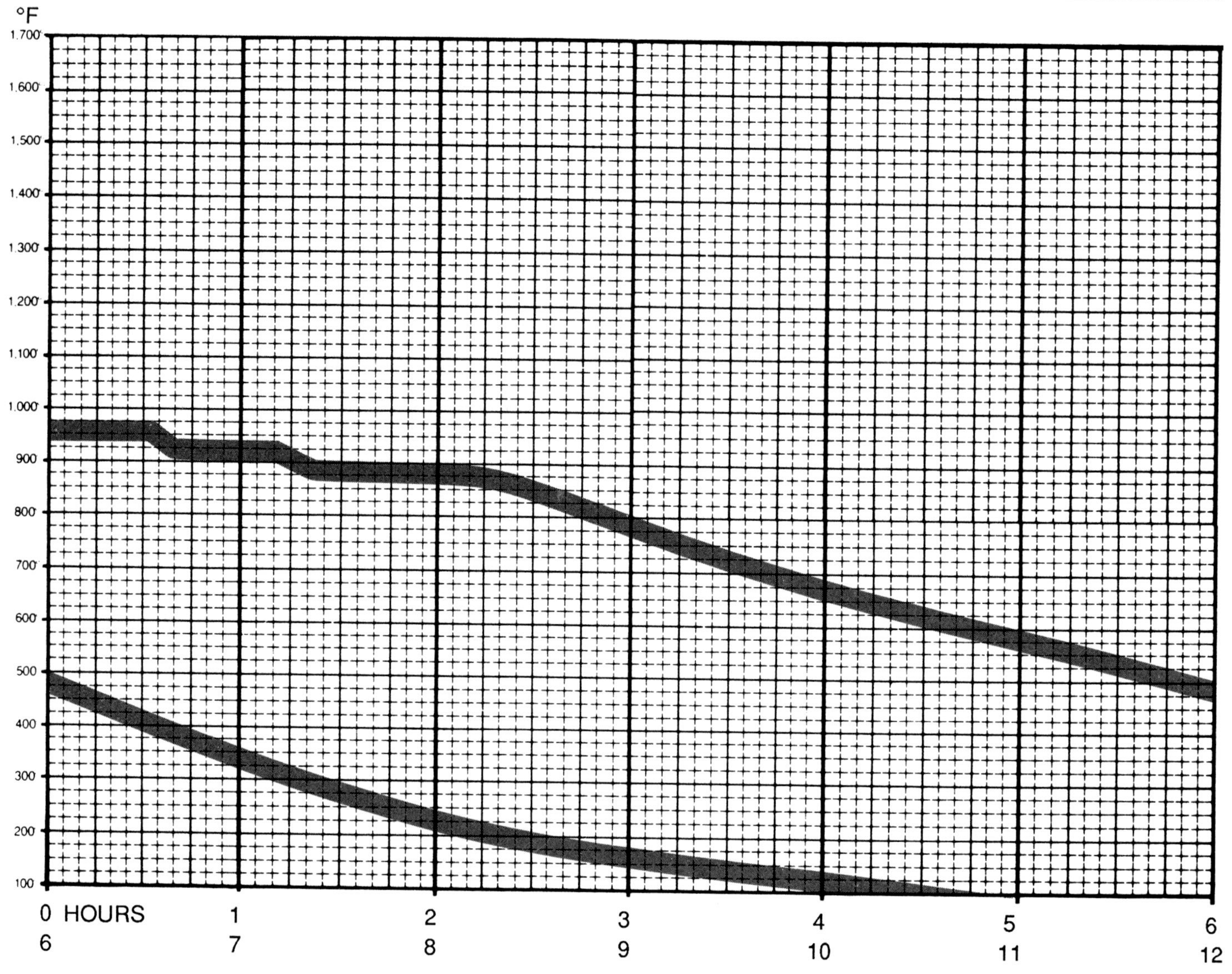

Annealing for 1/2" of glass.

I have found that it is prudent to divide the initial heating process into two stages: very slow rise to 350°F, then a somewhat more rapid rise to the strain point. Large pieces of glass, over 12" across, and tall stacks of glass, those four or more layers thick, should be heated at a rate of 7-10°F per minute. After this slow rise to approximately 350°F, a faster rate of 15-20°F per minute may be maintained up to the strain point. This rate of climb may be continued to the desired fusing temperature, or increased after reaching the strain point.

Heat soaking the glass at 1550°F (for Bullseye) for fifteen minutes gives more control of the surface line quality than does firing the kiln to a higher temperature for a shorter length of time. When the desired results are obtained, turn the kiln off and let it cool to the annealing temperature.

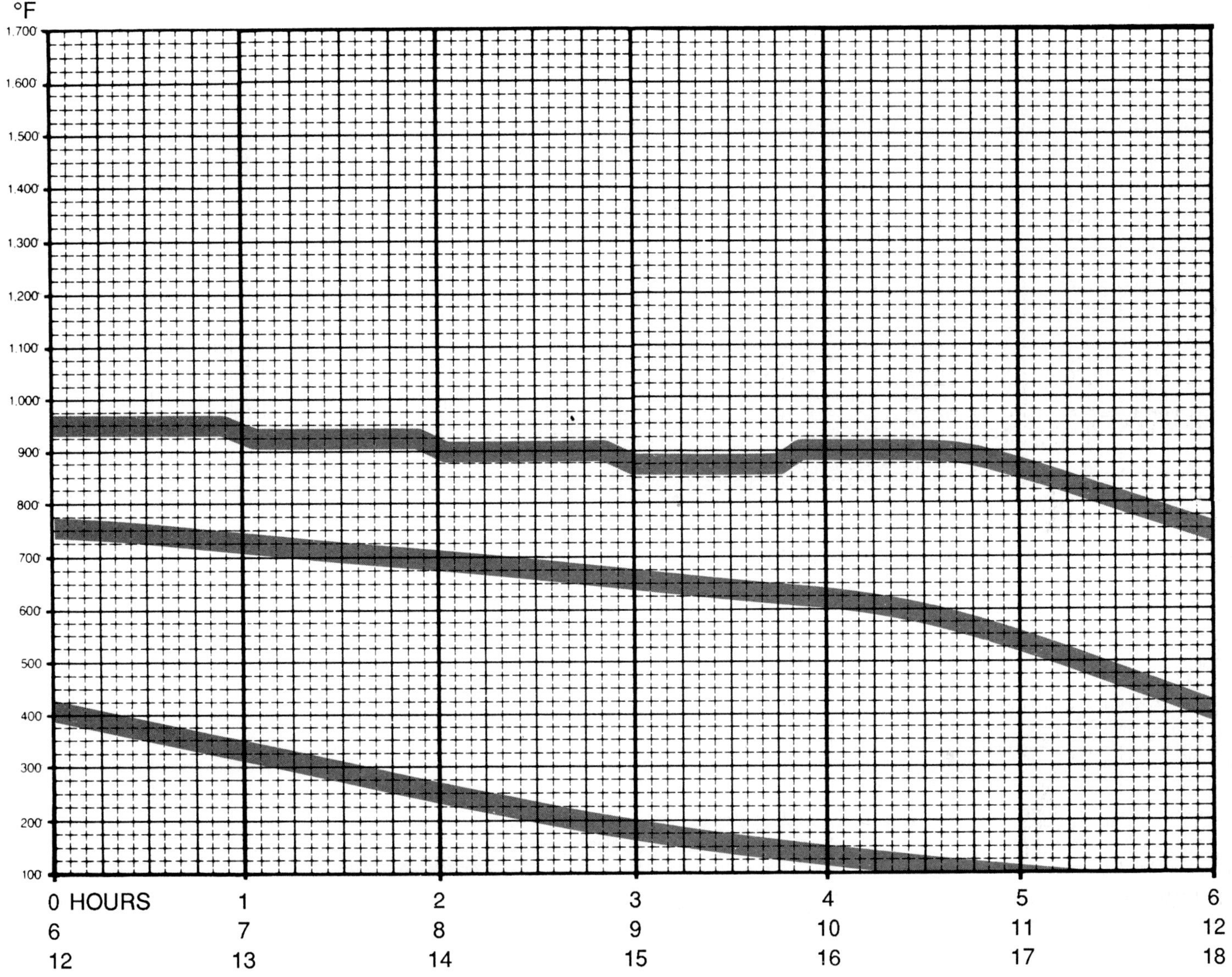

Heat treating for 1-1/2-2" cast glass.

Top loading kilns or kilns with a symmetrical venting system may be vented one-half inch, in order to speed cooling. But if the kiln cannot be cooled symmetrically, it is best to let it cool at its natural rate, with doors and peep holes closed. Venting a kiln unsymmetrically will cause a thermal gradient within the glass *and* the kiln that will cause uneven annealing.

The internal stress of any piece of glass depends on its thermal history, during cooling. A temperature gradient occurs whenever heat is conducted through any substance. As glass cools, the outside surface is always cooler than the inside. The thicker the glass and the larger the glass slab, the greater is this temperature difference. Heat soaking a slab of glass, within the annealing range, until the interior temperature is the same as the surface temperature, will remove the gradient, relieving the strain.

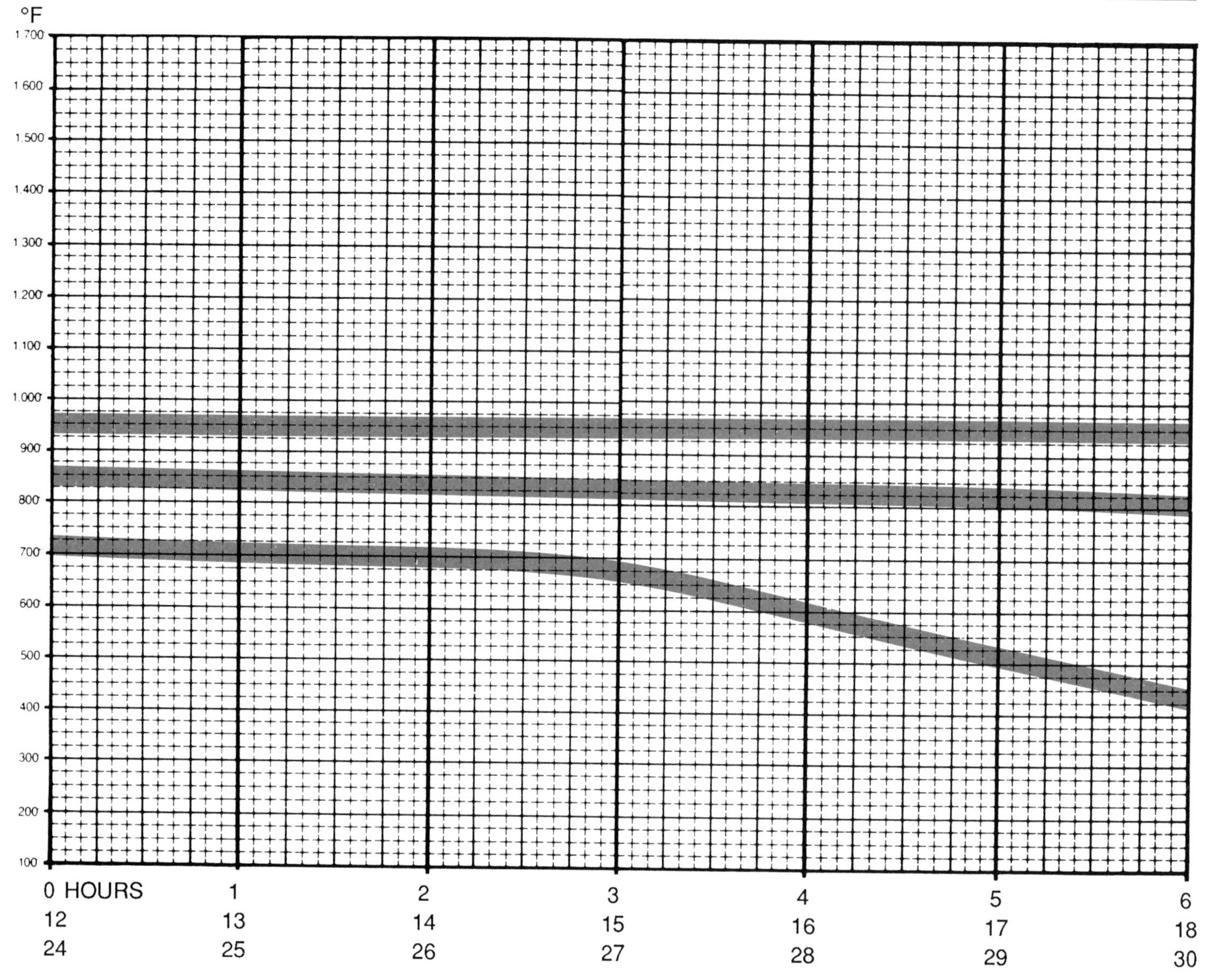

Graph shows theoretical annealing curve for 1" of glass

After heat soaking the glass at any temperature, it must be once again lowered in temperature, causing another thermal gradient. However, if most of the stress has been relieved by heat soaking and slow cooling through the annealing range to the strain point, it will be free of any permanent strain.

Any strain that occurs after the strain point will be temporary. If the cooling after the strain point proceeds at a uniform rate, there will be a constant temperature gradient between the surface of the glass and the middle of the glass. If the strain is not enough to break the glass during this cooling phase, from strain point to room temperature, and the entire slab becomes a uniform temperature, the temperature gradient disappears and so does the strain. As the glass slab approaches the size of the kiln shelf that supports it, the more likely it becomes that there will be a thermal gradient between the outside edges of the slab and the middle.

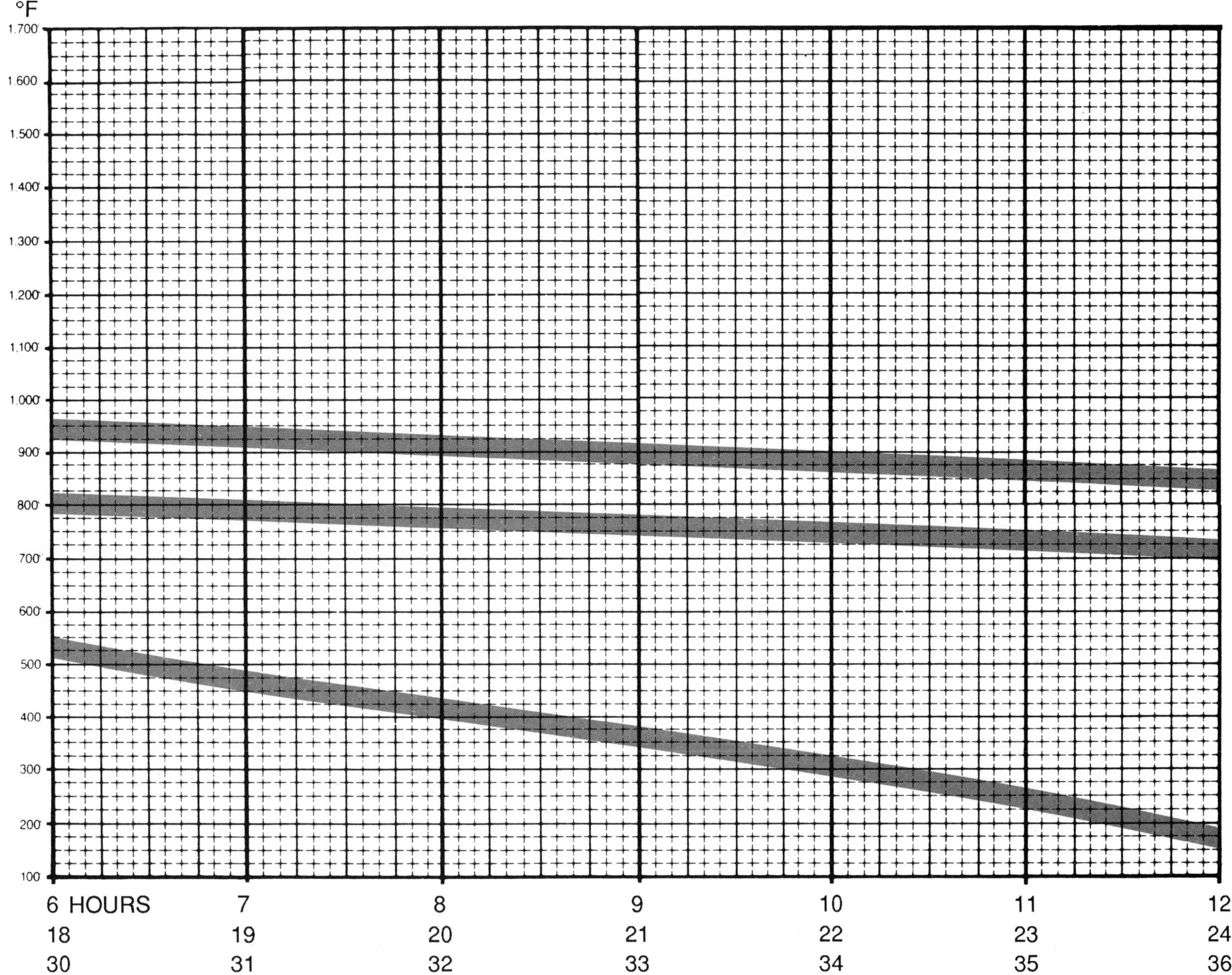

When these large pieces are annealed, heat must be added to the outside edges of the glass slab, not just over the top. For this reason it is important to have heating coils around the outside edges of the kiln shelf that supports the glass. In a side-fired kiln, the heat radiates from the side walls, where the elements are located, and goes toward the center of the kiln. The kiln shelf also conducts heat in this same direction, Therefore, the glass on the outer perimeter of the shelf receives heat before the glass in the center of the shelf does. Since the outside edges lose heat first during cooling, the ability to add heat to the edges during annealing is absolutely necessary when annealing glass slabs that are near the size of the kiln shelf, and as thick as one-half inch. Consequently, controlling heating elements independently for different areas of the kiln is critical when the glass fusing project is large and/or thick. The facility to have this control can, if necessary, be added to a kiln by installing a heating element just below the outer edge of the supporting kiln shelf.

TEMPERATURE CONVERSION TABLE

Find the temperature you want to convert, either °F or °C, in the center column of numbers. If the temperature is in °F, the figure to the left will be the correct temperature in °C; if the temperature is in °C, the figure to the right will be the correct termperature in °F.

°C		°F	°C		°F	°C		°F	°C		°F	°C		°F
			20.0	**68**	154.4	138	**280**	536	421	**790**	1454	704	**1300**	2372
			20.6	**69**	156.2	143	**290**	554	427	**800**	1472	710	**1310**	2390
			21.1	**70**	158.0	149	**300**	572	432	**810**	1490	716	**1320**	2408
			21.7	**71**	159.8	154	**310**	590	438	**820**	1508	721	**1330**	2426
			22.2	**72**	161.6	160	**320**	608	443	**830**	1526	727	**1340**	2444
			22.8	**73**	163.4	166	**330**	626	449	**840**	1544	732	**1350**	2462
			23.3	**74**	165.2	171	**340**	644	454	**850**	1562	738	**1360**	2480
			23.9	**75**	167.0	177	**350**	662	460	**860**	1580	743	**1370**	2498
			24.4	**76**	168.8	182	**360**	680	466	**870**	1598	749	**1380**	2516
			25.0	**77**	170.6	188	**370**	698	471	**880**	1616	754	**1390**	3534
			25.6	**78**	172.4	193	**380**	716	477	**890**	1634	760	**1400**	2552
			26.1	**79**	174.2	199	**390**	734	482	**900**	1652	766	**1410**	2570
			26.7	**80**	176.0	204	**400**	752	488	**910**	1670	771	**1420**	2588
			27.2	**81**	177.8	210	**410**	770	493	**920**	1688	777	**1430**	2606
			27.8	**82**	179.6	216	**420**	788	499	**930**	1706	782	**1440**	2624
0	**32**	89.6	28.3	**83**	181.4	221	**430**	806	504	**940**	1724	788	**1450**	2642
0.56	**33**	91.4	28.9	**84**	183.2	227	**440**	824	510	**950**	1742	793	**1460**	2660
1.11	**34**	93.2	29.4	**85**	185.0	232	**450**	842	516	**960**	1760	799	**1470**	2678
1.67	**35**	95.0	30.0	**86**	186.8	238	**460**	860	521	**970**	1778	804	**1480**	2696
2.22	**36**	96.8	30.6	**87**	188.6	243	**470**	878	527	**980**	1796	810	**1490**	2714
2.78	**37**	98.6	31.1	**88**	190.4	249	**480**	896	532	**990**	1814	816	**1500**	2732
3.33	**38**	100.4	31.7	**89**	192.2	254	**490**	914	538	**1000**	1832	821	**1510**	2750
3.89	**39**	102.2	32.2	**90**	194.0	260	**500**	932	543	**1010**	1850	827	**1520**	2768
4.44	**40**	104.0	32.8	**91**	195.8	266	**510**	950	549	**1020**	1868	832	**1530**	2786
5.00	**41**	105.8	33.3	**92**	197.6	271	**520**	968	554	**1030**	1886	838	**1540**	2804
5.56	**42**	107.6	33.9	**93**	199.4	277	**530**	986	560	**1040**	1904	843	**1550**	2822
6.11	**43**	109.4	34.4	**94**	201.2	282	**540**	1004	566	**1050**	1922	849	**1560**	2840
6.67	**44**	111.2	35.0	**95**	203.0	288	**550**	1022	571	**1060**	1940	854	**1570**	2858
7.22	**45**	113.0	35.6	**96**	204.8	293	**560**	1040	577	**1070**	1958	860	**1580**	2876
7.78	**46**	114.8	36.1	**97**	206.6	299	**570**	1058	582	**1080**	1976	866	**1590**	2894
8.33	**47**	116.6	36.7	**98**	208.4	304	**580**	1076	588	**1090**	1994	871	**1600**	2912
8.89	**48**	118.4	37.2	**99**	210.2	310	**590**	1094	593	**1100**	2012	877	**1610**	2930
9.44	**49**	120.2	38	**100**	212	316	**600**	1112	599	**1110**	2030	882	**1620**	2948
10.0	**50**	122.0	43	**110**	230	321	**610**	1130	604	**1120**	2048	888	**1630**	2966
10.6	**51**	123.8	49	**120**	248	327	**620**	1148	610	**1130**	2066	893	**1640**	2984
11.1	**52**	125.6	54	**130**	266	332	**630**	1166	616	**1140**	2084	899	**1650**	3002
11.7	**53**	127.4	60	**140**	284	338	**640**	1184	621	**1150**	2102	904	**1660**	3020
12.2	**54**	129.2	66	**150**	302	343	**650**	1202	627	**1160**	2120	910	**1670**	3038
12.8	**55**	131.0	71	**160**	320	349	**660**	1220	632	**1170**	2138	916	**1680**	3056
13.3	**56**	132.8	77	**170**	338	354	**670**	1238	638	**1180**	2156	921	**1690**	3074
13.9	**57**	134.6	82	**180**	356	360	**680**	1256	643	**1190**	2174	927	**1700**	3092
14.4	**58**	136.4	88	**190**	374	366	**690**	1274	649	**1200**	2192	932	**1710**	3110
15.0	**59**	138.2	93	**200**	392	371	**700**	1292	654	**1210**	2210	938	**1720**	3128
15.6	**60**	140.0	99	**210**	410	377	**710**	1310	660	**1220**	2228	943	**1730**	3146
16.1	**61**	141.8	100	**212**	413	382	**720**	1328	666	**1230**	2246	949	**1740**	3164
16.7	**62**	143.6	104	**220**	428	388	**730**	1346	671	**1240**	2264	954	**1750**	3182
17.2	**63**	145.4	110	**230**	446	393	**740**	1364	677	**1250**	2282	960	**1760**	3200
17.8	**64**	147.2	116	**240**	464	399	**750**	1382	682	**1260**	2300	966	**1770**	3218
18.3	**65**	149.0	121	**250**	482	404	**760**	1400	688	**1270**	2318	971	**1780**	3236
18.9	**66**	150.8	127	**260**	500	410	**770**	1418	693	**1280**	2336	977	**1790**	3254
19.4	**67**	152.6	132	**270**	518	416	**780**	1436	699	**1290**	2354	982	**1800**	3272

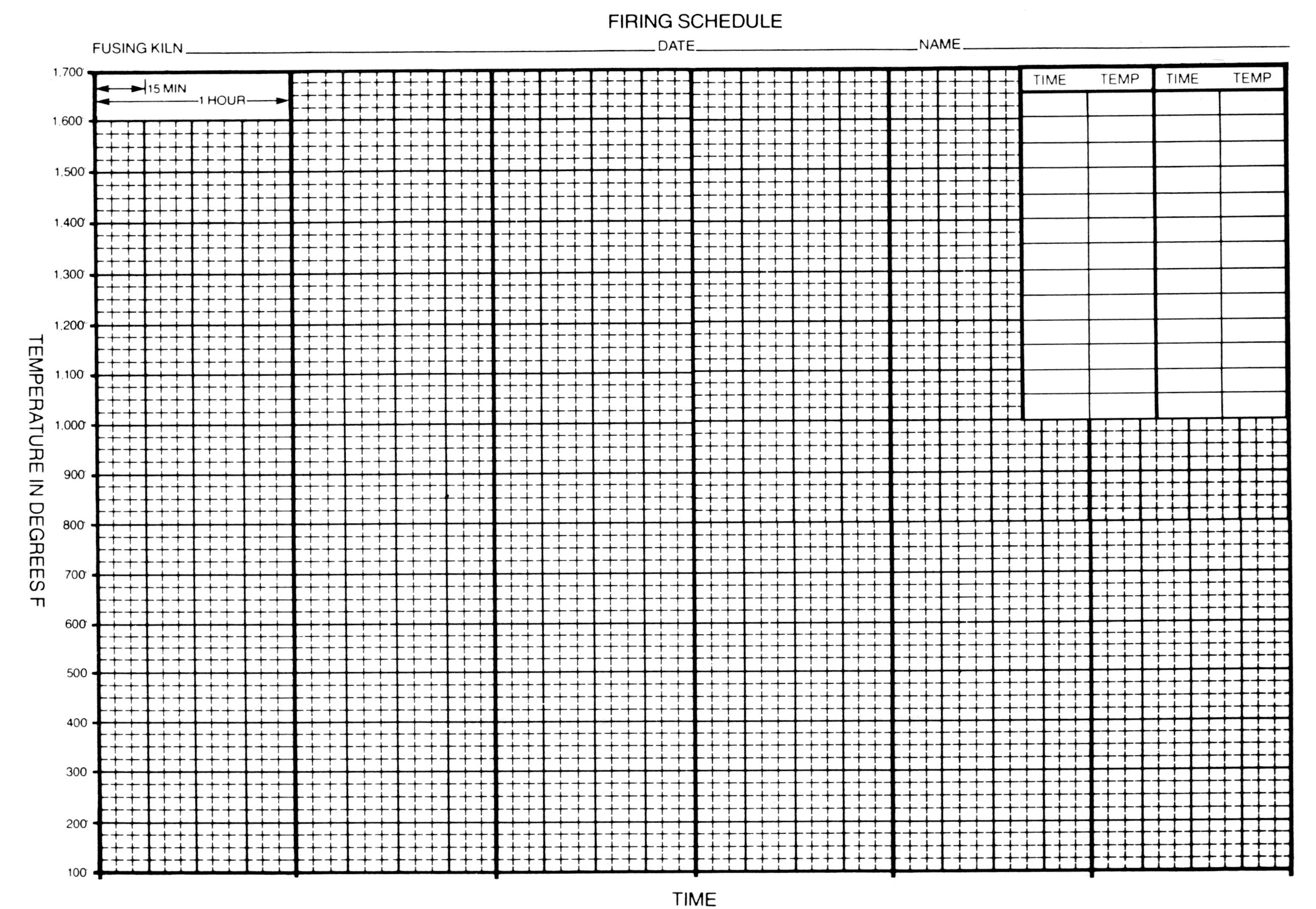
FIRING SCHEDULE
FUSING KILN
DATE
NAME
TIME
TEMP
TIME
TEMP
15 MIN
1 HOUR
1,700
1,600
1,500
1,400
1,300
1,200
1,100
1,000
900
800
700
600
500
400
300
200
100
TEMPERATURE IN DEGREES F
TIME

TECHNICAL ASPECTS OF FUSING WITH BULLSEYE GLASS

by Daniel Schwoerer
President, Bullseye Glass Company

KILNFORMED GLASS

Having co-authored a book a number of years ago that attempted to present some of the myriad possibilities available to anyone willing to reheat sheet glass, I hope now to be able to clarify and expand on some of the basic techniques presented there and to provide a little more information which will be of use to those who work with our glass in one of the numerous methods broadly categorized as "kilnforming". I feel also somewhat responsible to clear up a certain confusion of terminology resulting from publishing a book entitled *Glass Fusing Book 1* that addressed procedures rather broader in scope than the term "fusing" alone implies.

In its strictest definition glass fusing refers to the heat bonding of glasses. In its recent resurgence *fusing* has been loosely used to describe a wide variety of techniques involving the viscous manipulation of previously formed pieces of glass in a kiln. The glass may range from chunks of cullet to crushed, fritted or cut pieces of flat sheet glass to previously fused glass elements or forms. The procedures involving these materials may be done on flat kiln shelves, into or over molds. The degree to which the glasses are fused can vary from a low heat in which they are just tacked together, to a high heat in which they become a flowing liquid. Considering the diversity of techniques and materials involved, the term *kilnforming* would seem to more acurately describe this exceedingly broad area of glassworking.

FUSING

As a specific heat treatment of glass, fusing occurs over a broad temperature range with end results that are visually quite varied. At the lowest heat possible, fused glass pieces will stick together (the term "laminating" or "tack fusing" is frequently applied here), but retain almost all of their initial physical characteristics save a slight rounding of edges. At this heat level no noticeable flow or displacement of the individual pieces of glass occurs.

In fusing at higher heats, the separate pieces of glass completely lose their original shapes, flowing together, eliminating voids or spaces between them. Techniques at this heat level include indirect crucible pouring, direct mold casting, pate de verre etc.

Between these two extremes the possibilities for fusing pieces of preformed glass are virtually limitless.

COMPATIBILITY

To successfully fuse two or more glasses together all of the glasses need to be *compatible*. Compatibility is the characteristic of certain glasses that allows them to be fused together and — after proper cooling to room temperature — have no undue stresses that will lead to fracturing. The tendency of many colored glasses to be *incompatible* with each other has always been a major obstacle in fusing.

Compatibility requires that the various glasses expand and contract similarly upon heating or cooling. More technically stated, the glasses must have similar *coefficients of expansion*.. The coefficient of expansion is a number that expresses a percentage of change in length per degree of change in temperature. The coefficient of expansion is determined by measuring the change in length of glass for a one degree centigrade increase in temperature. (Fig 1). It is obviously a very small number (Bullseye glasses are in the vicinity of 0.0000090). For simplicity's sake when comparing expansion coefficients of different glasses, all the zeros are ignored. Bullseye glass is commonly referred to as having an expansion of approximately "90".

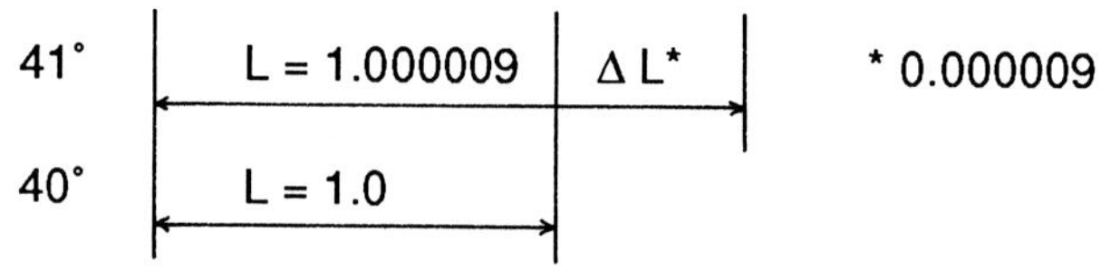

41°	L = 1.000009	Δ L*	* 0.000009
40°	L = 1.0		

Fig. 1 Coefficient of Expansion $= \frac{\Delta L}{L} = \frac{.000009}{1} = 90 \times 10^{-7} / C°$

The magnitude of the expansion number is a relative measure of how much a particular glass expands upon heating. The larger the number, the greater the expansion. Lower expansion glasses have better resistance to thermal shock. Pyrex (32.5), for example, will withstand a direct flame, while higher expansion glasses (those generally above 100) similar to many studio blowing glasses are more susceptible to shock and will not hold up well when subjected to temperature changes such as those experienced in repeated cycles of a dishwasher.

MEASUREMENTS OF EXPANSION

Unfortunately, most laboratory tests used to determine coefficients of expansion are performed over a temperature range from room temperature to 300°C (512° F). In fusing, the expansion from 300° C upward to the softening point is as important as the expansion in the lower range. In fact, the expansion above the strain point is usually 2 to 3 times greater than that below the strain point and in many cases this expansion rate is quite non-linear. This explains why laboratory determinations of expansions cannot necessarily be used as the sole criteria of compatibility for fusing.

Similarly, theoretical coefficients of expansion which are determined by mathematical formulas such as those of English and Turner can be extremely inaccurate when applied to formulas other than those of simple soda-lime glasses. Because calculations of this type are based on very specific ingredients and do not take into account variations in raw materials, melting schedules or the high percentages of various coloring oxides the results they yield when applied to complex glasses are frequently quite skewed.

For instance, English and Turner's calculations when applied to Bullseye's clear (#1101) and white opalescent (#0113) glasses yield coefficients of expansion of 84.5 and 76.5 respectively. The measured coefficients for these glasses are in fact 91 and 88. It is important to note that these glasses show no stress when tested for compatibility under conditions duplicating those of the actual fusing process.

CHIP TEST FOR COMPATIBILITY

The most relevant test for fusing compatibility anticipates and attempts to duplicate the same process that will be used in producing the final fused piece. Bullseye has employed this testing method for the last 9 years in generating its line of "Tested Compatible" glasses. The method is an adaptation of that used regularly in the technical glass community while incorporating the actual fusing process. I refer to it as the *chip test*.

Chips of colored glass approximately 1/2" square are fused to a larger base strip (we use strips 2" x 14") of clear glass. A control chip of the same base clear glass is also fused to the bar as a test of adequate annealing. (Annealing being the process of controlled cooling of the glass to avoid undesireable stresses in the final cold state.) After proper annealing the chips are viewed with a polariscope. Stress existing between the colored chip and the base clear glass will appear as a halo of light surrounding the chip. The intensity of the halo is a qualitative measure of the amount of stress. (See appendix A for more details). If little or no halo is evident, the glasses are compatible or "fit". All glasses which fit the same clear base glass will fit each other.

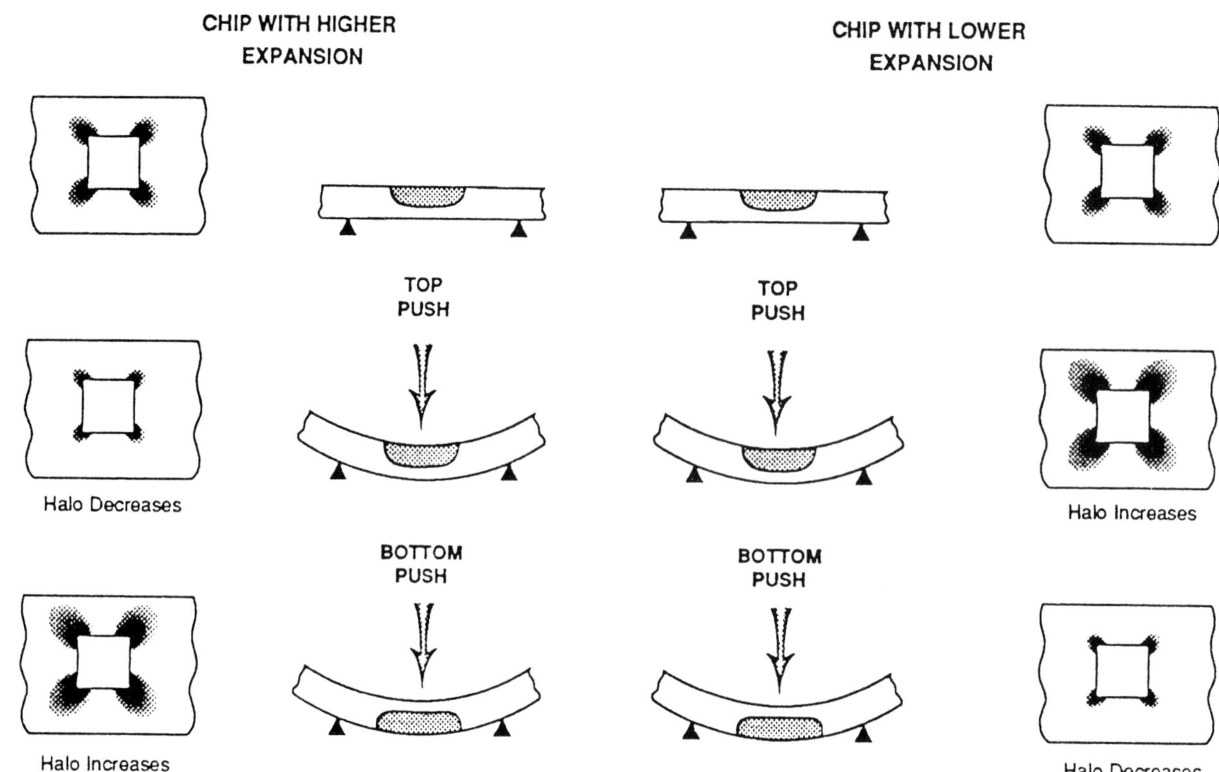

Fig.2: Procedure to determine whether chip glass is higher or lower in expansion than surrounding glass

In addition to compatibility information the chip test will reveal any color changes that may take place on re-firing of the glass, as well as the relative softening and flow characteristics. Additionally, a determination can be made as to whether the tested chip is higher or lower in expansion than the base clear glass by applying downward pressure on the chip and observing the change in intensity of the halo as described in Figure 2 above.

At Bullseye we have for a number of years accepted, marked and sold as "Tested Compatible" only those glasses which showed *no halo at all* in our factory compatibility testing. This does not mean that glasses showing slight stress or haloing will not work perfectly adequately for most fusing applications. By maintaining standards higher than are generally necessary we have tried to safeguard against any slight variations that might occur over time both in our own production or in the studio fuser's use of our glass. We have attempted to maintain a standardized clear glass which could be used for testing of all our other glasses and which would remain constant in succeeding years, insuring compatibility not only between sheets and runs, but year after year. I believe our success in accomplishing this goal is attested to by the number of artists who have regularly and successfully used our glasses in kilnforming applications over the last 9 years.

TOLERANCES OF STRESS

If, however, a *total* absence of haloing or stress in compatibility testing is not necessary for most successful fusing procedures, what are in fact the allowable tolerances?

Acceptable levels of stress whether related to compatibility or annealing should be determined by consideration of the following:

• *The size & thickness of the finished piece.*

The tolerances for jewelry work will clearly be much greater than those acceptable when fusing multi-layered constructions 20" in diameter.

• *Any secondary processing which will later be done to the work.*

If the work is to be sandblasted, ground, carved or otherwise subjected to surface abrasion it will be less able to tolerate stress.

• *The object's intended use.*

Objects which will be used in a functional way, subjected to frequent handling or repeated temperature changes will need to be freer of stress than those destined for the gallery or museum collection.

ANNEALING

The successful annealing of Bullseye's glasses, like the successful annealing of all glasses, is largely dependant upon the 3 points noted above. Annealing, however, —unlike compatibility — is affected by a 4th variable: the kilnforming procedures and conditions which precede and/or accompany it. For instance, if the kilnforming process involves uneven heating or cooling of the glass surface such as occurs in crash cooling the kiln to "freeze a shape" the glass may need to be soaked at a higher heat before proceeding with the annealing schedule. Or if the glass has been formed in a massive mold the heat transfer between the mold and the glass may require altering the annealing schedule.

Annealing schedules should be determined not only by the glass, its composition, size, end-use, and cold-working eventualities, but also by the size and configuration of the kiln or lehr in which the controlled cooling will occur.

In order to determine a proper annealing cycle certain technical data relating to the glass is necessary. These are: the softening, annealing, and strain points of the glass. For two typical Bullseye glasses the relevant technical data (and coefficients of expansion) are as follows:

	1101F Clear	**0113F White opalescent**
Softening point:	1260˚F	1270˚F
Annealing point:	990˚	935˚
Strain point:	920˚	865˚
Measured coefficient of expansion (0-300˚C):	91	88

The information above enables us to compute an accurate annealing cycle by indicating the rate of release of stress at various temperatures in the annealing region.

It is difficult for stress to exist above the softening point since the glass quickly flows to relieve it. As glass cools it becomes stiffer and hence cannot relieve stress as easily by flowing. At the annealing point any stresses existing in the glass can be relieved in minutes. At the strain point, however, it will take hours to relieve the same stresses. *Below* the strain point stresses in the glass will not be relieved over any length of time.

From this it would appear best to soak at the annealing point for a short time and cool slowly down through the strain point to room temperature.

In practice, however, it is best to anneal by soaking the glass for a much longer time somewhere well below the annealing point but above the strain point, cool very slowly to some temperature well below the strain point and then cool to room temperature.

Recommended annealing schedules for various thicknesses of Bullseye glasses are given in table 1. The table was developed directly from information available in *The Glass Engineering Handbook*, 3rd Edition by McLellan and Shand (Chapter 4, "Stress Release and Annealing")

Thick-ness	Soak Temp	Soak Time	First Cooling Stage (Maximum)	2nd Cooling Stage (Maximum)	Final Cooling to Room Temp (Max)	Total Time
1/8"	930°F	1 Hr	7° / min to 855°F	14° / min to 765°F	20° / min	1 Hr 50 min
1/4"	930°	2 Hrs	2° / min to 845°	4° / min to 755°	20° / min	3 Hrs 39 min
1/2"	930°	4 Hrs	0.5°/min to 825°	1° / min to 735°	5° / min	11 Hrs 12 min
1"	930°	8 Hrs	0.15°/min to 785°	0.3°/min to 695°	1° / min	39 Hrs 27 min

Table 1: Annealing Schedules for Bullseye Glass

It is necessary to keep in mind that the annealing schedules given in Table 1 are what the *glass* should experience. It is necessary to take into account the difference between the glass temperature and kiln temperature during firing. As a general rule (with variations specific to each kiln and firing schedule) the temperature of the glass will be 50°F lower than the air temperature of the kiln on heat up and 50°F hotter than the air temperature on cool down.

In the final analysis there are no pre-determined schedules which can take into account all the variables involved when firing Bullseye or any other glass. However, given the information detailed above, an awareness of his/her own equipment, and a systematic approach to observation and record-keeping, the kilnworker should have little difficulty in successfully fusing and annealing Bullseye.

To quote Paul Marioni: "Annealing formulas are like bread recipes — everyone has one."

Appendix A
MECHANICS OF CHIP STRESS TEST

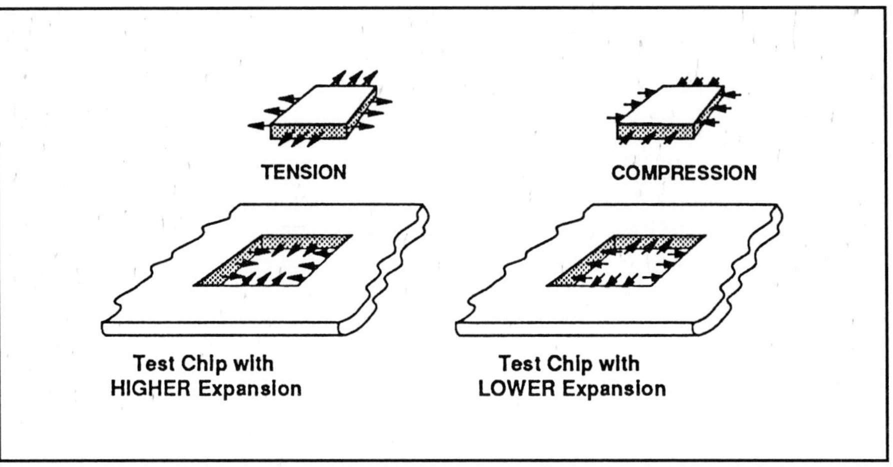

A chip of colored glass with a higher expansion will shrink **more** than the surrounding clear glass. This will cause both the colored chip as well as the surrounding clear glass to be in tension at the interface of each.

Likewise, a chip of colored glass with a lower expansion will shrink **less** than the surrounding clear glass, creating compression at the interface of each.

The tension or compression will cause halos of light to appear at the interface of the chip and the base glass when viewed with a polariscope.

The test appears to be more sensitive to measurements of tension than those of compression. The accuracy of the test is probably + 1 expansion point when the chip is of a higher expansion and + 2 points when the chip is of a lower expansion.

For further information refer to *The Handbook of Glass Manufacture Vol II* by Dr. Fay V. Tooley, Section 14 “Annealing and Tempering”.

ANNOTATED RESOURCE INDEX

Anderson, Harriette, *Kiln Fired Glass*, Chilton Books, Ontario, 1970

Out of print, but still fairly easy to find in used book stores and many libraries, this book contains many useful ideas and possible directions for the hobbyist. Anderson writes of her personal experiences with the use of enamels.

Arwas, Victor, *Glass-Art Nouveau-Art Deco*, Abrams, Inc., New York, 1987

This is an historical book covering the background of glass artists and their techniques from the late 1800's to 1940. Daum, Galle, Lalique, Marinot, Tiffany, and others are discussed in detail. It contains over 250 color pictures, including photos of works from private collections not usually seen in other publications.

Bloch-Dermant, *The Art of French Glass*, Viking, New York, 1974

This book is similar to the Arwas book, above, but not as broad in scope. Excellent photographs, 118 of which are in color. This book is full of detailed and technical information on France's leading artist-glassmakers. It is written simply and directly. The last chapter on pate de verre offers historical and technical insights into this glass process.

Cummings, Keith, *The Technique of Glass Forming*, B.T. Batsford, LTD, London, 1980

Out of print, but worth a look, if you can find it, Cummings' was the first visually stimulating book on kiln forming glass. The section on press forming glass with a wooden mold, and then slumping over a form, is complete and makes the process inviting. Cummings covers glass art history, providing photos of the work, followed by an expose of how, in his view, the glass pieces were made.

Denoel, *La Pate De Verre*, Editions Denoel, Paris, 1984

This book is a visual feast of traditional French pate de verre work. Although I have not read a translation of the French text, I find the work put together in this book worthwhile. Many of the photos are of work not seen in other publications, and 40% of the photos are in color.

Duthie, Arthur, *Decorative Glass Processes*, Corning Museum/Dover, New York , 1982

Originally published in 1911, this book was the first comprehensive volume on flat glass decorative processes that was written in English. It was reprinted by the Corning Museum of Glass in appreciation of its excellence. It is amazing to read a book by a skilled craftsman writing 80 years ago, who seems as you read his work, to be a contemporary. The sections on patents and "recent" developments of sandblasting and electroplating are both interesting and comical.

Glasses, Borax Consolidated Limited, London, 1965

This small book was written by Borax Consolidated Ltd. to explain how boric oxide is used in the composition of a wide range of glasses. It explains glass forming technology in a way that a novice can understand. Batch recipes and glass materials are listed. Melting procedures are described simply. The methods of forming glass containers, fiberglass, and technical glasses are explained with excellent illustrations. This is absolutely the best written book on industrial glass chemistry and forming methods available. This book was written as a sales tool and information guide for the glass industry. It can be obtained by writing to Borax Consolidated Limited, Borax House, Carlisle Place, London, England, SW1P 1HT

Hodkin, F.W., *A Textbook of Glass Technology*, Van Nostrand Reinhold, New York,1927

This is a reference book on the chemistry of glass, and industrial forming techniques. Although it has been out of print for sixty years, it can still be found in some reference libraries.

Goldstein, Sidney, *Pre-Roman and Early Roman Glass in The Corning Museum of Glass*, Corning Museum, Corning, New York, 1979

There is no better resource for insight into the forming methods used by the Romans than the first ten pages of this book. The balance of the book is a picture reference guide to glass in the Corning Museum.

Illustrated Science and Invention Encyclopedia, H.S. Stuttman Co., New York, 1977

The section on glass has the most complete illustrations and explanation that I have found on the float glass forming process.

Lalique Glass, Corning Museum/ Dover, New York, 1981

This is an excellent pictorial survey of this most important glass factory. Looking at the accomplishments of Lalique makes one feel rather insignificant, but also challenged. Included are photos of some of the best cast crystal glass work I have seen.

Le Blanc, Raymond, *Gold Leaf Techniques*, Third edition, St. Publications, Cincinnati, Ohio, 1986

This was written for sign painters, and is the most complete text available on the subject of gold leaf. This book is a great help to the glass artist who wants to use gold in conjunction with glass.

Lundstrom and Schwoerer, *Glass Fusing Book One,* Vitreous Publications, Portland, Oregon, 1983

Now here's a book! This is still the most accurate and comprehensive material available on basic glass fusing.

Masterpieces of Glass, Corning Museum/Abrams, Inc, New York, 1980

This is an excellent historical survey in one volume.

Pfaender, Heinz, *Schott Guide to Glass*, Van Nostrand Reinhold, New York, 1983

This book explains the fundamentals of glass: what it is made of, how it is made, and how it has been used. It is a complete reference on all modern applications of glass processes and uses, and includes information on obscure topics such as sealing glass, conductive glass, foam glass, and potential future uses of glass.

Reynolds, Gil, *The Fused Glass Handbook*, Fusion Headquarters, Portland, Oregon, 1987

As a book directed to the hobbyist, it has simple, easy to follow directions.

Scholes, Samuel, *Modern Glass Practice*, Cahners Publishing, Boston, 1975

This technical book is the number two reference, in my regard, on glass composition and melting. Written as a text book for students in glass technology, it begins with the elementary physics of the glassy state, then continues through the chemistry of glass color and composition, mixing batch, furnaces, melting, and annealing.

Schuler, Frederick and Lilli, *Glassforming*, Chilton, Philadelphia, 1970

This work covers flame working, enamels, glass color, and mold forming of glass in an easy to understand way. The reader may wish there were more information on each process. The technical information on glass is very complete, but the forming techniques and the examples used are very basic.

Schultes and Davis, *The Glass Flowers at Harvard*, E.P. Dutton, New York, 1982

The flowers in this collection are unbelievable and, as a reference, the book provides an idea of what kind of detail can be accomplished with the lampworking process.

Shand, E.B., *Glass Engineering Handbook*, McGraw-Hill, New York, 1958

This is the number one reference book on glass formulation, melting, and annealing. It is an excellent reference, but may put you to sleep.

Vargin V.V., *Technology of Enamels*, Hart, Inc., New York

Translated from the Russian, this is the most complete book on enamel technology that I know of. It can be hard to understand unless you have a background in chemistry. It gives excellent information on making enamels fit other materials. Although the book is out of print, it can be found in reference libraries.

Weyl, W.A., *Coloured Glasses*, Sheffield, 1951

This is a very technical book, the best around on coloring glass. To benefit fully from its contents, one needs to have a masters degree in glass chemistry, but the novice glass melter may get some good ideas about glass colors.

Education at Camp Colton

These days we seem to talk about The Glass Program at Camp Colton. Yet the camp had a long and illustrious history before it was ever invaded by anyone with glass madness. Before we bought the camp, it had a 55 year history as a Lutheran children's camp, also used for 4-H and outdoor school. Anyone who experienced its delights never forgot the name or the place that brought them such inspiration. I was one of those who was so affected. And so were my grandfather, my father and my son.

When I was old enough to travel to Oregon from California to visit my grandparents in Colton, my granddad frequently took me to the camp to experience the wonders there that delighted him. He and the other early members of Colton Lutheran Church had toiled to make the beautiful place by the creeks into a strong organization camp.

For the years between 1980 and 1984 I was a traveling minister of glass fusing. I seemed to be asked once every few weeks to travel to Maryland or Georgia or Australia or Japan to tell people how to fuse glass. When Kathy and I bought Camp Colton in 1985, to save it from the destruction that would have been inevitable at the hands of those who saw it as ready for development as real estate, we felt it would take nearly every minute at home (at camp) to find ourselves equal to the task of bringing the camp back to usefulness. We decided to find out if people would like to come to western Oregon and stay in one its most beautiful settings, while learning all the aspects of the craft of glass fusing. And so began The Glass Program at Camp Colton.

Kathy has occasionally gotten the award for most successful "firings" during a session.

Since that decision was made, we have been enlightened and exhausted and delighted by a continuing stream of student guests from all over the world. Our classes are held at various times of the year, but not at all times of the year. We have never stopped being amazed at the diversity within the groups we host. The individuals vary widely in age—from 22 to 80, with an average age in the mid-forties. They are equally diverse in background and degree of experience with glass. And I find it hard to think of any one of them who didn't have something special to give the group that convened here, and to us! Our sessions are quite small, and each group seems to become a family during the stay.

The Glass Program at Camp Colton is designed to bring students together in a situation where they can discover the materials and equipment available, learn the technology and sources for these, and prepare themselves to use that information to implement their own goals for designing with glass. Classes are outlined and structured so that a large body of knowledge can be covered. The teachers are people who love sharing a knowledge base and know how to communicate. The Glass Program at Camp Colton strives to provide a solid background in kiln fired glass, which can be built upon by the individual.

Camp Colton is thirty-five miles southeast of Portland, Oregon, in the Mt. Hood foothills. It consists of fifty-six acres of beautifully wooded land with two ponds (where I raise trout) and two streams. The trees are Douglas firs, some over 200 feet tall, and Western red cedar, mixed with a pleasant smattering of deciduous Alders and Maples. There seems to be about the place an essence that speaks, even to newcomers, of its history and the integrity of its founders. All this makes for an unusually pleasant setting, no doubt about it. But it is also freeing and serene and the students respond accordingly.

Boyce watches a six-pound trout follow his fly.

During their stay our student guests occupy small, sparsely furnished rooms, in the sunny, open area next to the lake. They respond to the old dinner bell for their meals, served in Riverfalls Lodge, located at the juncture of the two creeks. The glass seems to tempt them to spend long hours in the studios, but we manage to lure them outdoors for hikes, trout fishing, bowling ball croquet, evening campfires, and frequent pre-dinner horseshoe games.

Our students discover that we have reason to be as proud of our meal service as we are of the depth of the glass education we provide. We have focused with success on serving unusual, healthful, attractive menus. They are carefully prepared from natural foods, include homemade breads and desserts, and emphasize local foods including, of course, our own trout.

While lecture hours are specific, individual work proceeds at any pace that suits the individual. With the particular combination of facilities, the small size of our groups, the style of our meals, and the flexibility of the class work, we find we have been able to make students of all ages and levels of experience and energy comfortable. The goal, after all, is to help those individuals pursue the knowledge base they need to advance in their work. And we know that the glass education available at Camp Colton is well designed to do just that.

About the Author

I began working with glass in 1965, when I joined the new glass program established by Dr. Robert Fritz that year at San Jose State University in San Jose, California. At that time I was a ceramics major, studying with one of the great ceramic glaze technicians of our time, Dr. Herbert Sanders. The close correlation between the calculating and making of ceramic glazes and the process of making glass is a natural one. So, as a potter studying glaze calculation, I found it natural to apply the technology to glass, and was soon drawn by the material.

Dr. Fritz introduced glass and glass blowing as a medium for art. He put special emphasis on learning the nature and behavior of different glasses. His program matured over three years to the point that each individual student could learn to control all phases of the process of making finished blown objects. We built glass melting equipment, calculated and melted batch, formed the glass, and carried out all the cold working processes for finishing the annealed work. This, my introduction to glass, has never been forgotten, and my desire since then has been to share as much with others interested in glass as Robert Fritz did with me.

After my graduation from San Jose State, in 1967, I set up a ceramics and glass studio in southern California, teaching and selling my work there for two years until my wife and I moved to Corvallis, Oregon, in late 1969. At that time, in fulfillment of alternative service for the United States Government, I set up a ceramics and glass program for the Children's Farm Home, near Corvallis.

At the end of two years alternative service, I organized a home blowing studio in Corvallis, where I blew glass for galleries and craft fairs. While participating in craft fairs and shows, I met many other glass artists who had become infatuated with hot glass in the early years of the studio blowing movement in this country. We were all struggling to support our individual studios and families, while experimenting with new glasses and equipment.

Two of those artists were Ray Ahlgren and Dan Schwoerer, who were partners in a glass blowing studio in Portland, Oregon. It seemed that their experience and love for glass were similar to my own. Our experience in the glass world pointed to a need for more colored sheet glass for the stained glass industry. Forming a partnership in 1974, we established Bullseye Glass Company, the first new glass manufacturer to produce opal sheet glass since 1900.

For the next four years the pressing demands of an infant company consumed all of my time. As the company president in charge of administration and sales, I had little time for creative work. However, in 1978 I began designing independent stained glass panels, executed for me by more capable craftspersons. Although I completed a relatively large body of work, I was unsatisfied with the black lines and the cartoon effect created by the lead and copper foil. Even though I had control of the colors and texture of all the glass I used (I could make my own glass in the factory), I was not happy with the results.

I had met Kay Kinney during my years in southern California, and was aware of her struggles with fusing and laminating glass. In books I saw ancient Egyptian fusing, as well as fused work by contemporary artists Michael and Frances Higgins and Maurice Heaton. Since, at Bullseye, we produced mixed colors of glass daily, and had control of the formulas, it seemed a foregone conclusion that we could make sheet glass with similar coefficients of expansion.

The thought process went something like this: if sheet glasses had the same coefficient of expansion, they could be cut into shapes and fused together and there would be no need for all those cartoon lines. So, I started experimenting in 1979 or 1980—I don't know exactly when because the process was slow at first, fraught with many failures and just a few successes. If there was one memorable breakthrough, it was the application of the method of testing for stress with a polarimeter (from glass blowing) to glasses fused to a clear sheet glass with a constant coefficient of expansion.

When making sheet glass it is not important to have a constant coefficient of expansion among all the glasses. Single colors can all be different and mixed colors only have to be within one or two coefficient points of one another. In glass blowing it is not uncommon to use glasses together that vary in coefficient of expansion by four or five points, because the casing process holds the glass together. But when fusing glass flat, the glasses must be very close in coefficients. Establishing a clear glass as a constant, and then formulating the melt for all colors to fit that constant, made the contemporary glass fusing movement possible.

The ability to fuse glass, by taking it through the complete process of heating, holding and annealing, then checking the finished results with an accurate test, really stimulated my dreams of unlimited possibilities. I saw kiln fired glass as the wave of the future, providing freedom for all those who would like to be freed of the lead lines! Tiles, windows, bowls, sculptures, and building faces could all be made with fused sheet glass.

By 1981 I became adamant about producing glass for the fusing market at Bullseye Glass. My remaining partner, Dan Schwoerer, supported me in my one-man campaign to make fusing available to everyone, and during the next few years we succeeded in making available a line of fusing compatible glasses, teaching fusing in diverse parts of the world, establishing a line of products, besides glass, that fusers needed for their work, working with kiln manufacturers to get kilns designed for glass on the market, and writing *Glass Fusing Book One.*

The market was slow to move toward my vision for the fusing movement, and all that energy took its toll in a company whose focus remained the production of quality hand rolled sheet glass. In 1985, at the same time that Camp Colton came into our lives, I sold my shares of Bullseye to Dan, who keeps the company on track, making the best sheet glass they can make, leaving me free to concentrate on those questions that concern glass fusing.

Whereas the material glass continues to fascinate me, so much of what I do is stimulated by other people. My students and my friends in the glass art world have always challenged me with their questions and provided help in testing my theories.

NOTES

PUBLICATIONS ORDER FORM

GLASS FUSING BOOK ONE	History and Contemporary Work • Basic Fusing Techniques • Compatibility • Firing and Annealing • Tools & Kilns • Molds • Slumping • Finishing Processes	_____ **@ $30.00 =** _______
PROJECTS IN KILN FIRED GLASS	A Set of Four Project Packets, Including Patterns, which Teach Specific Fusing Lessons: Wire Inclusions • Use of Glue • Stacking Methods • Production Work • Slumping • Pattern Placement	_____ **@ $10.00 =** _______
ADVANCED FUSING TECHNIQUES **Glass Fusing Book Two**	Bas Relief • Fiber Paper • Glory Hole • Sagging and Slumping • Designing • Using Stringer • Enamels and Lusters • Iridizing • Safety	_____ **@ $40.00 =** _______
GLASS CASTING AND MOLDMAKING **Glass Fusing Book Three**	Pate de Verre • Metal, Clay and Sand Molds • Kiln Forming in Sand • Lost Wax Casting • Castable Mold Materials and Formulas • Crucible Furnaces • Fiber Molds	_____ **@ $40.00 =** _______
SHIPPING, DOMESTIC, EACH BOOK OR PROJECT SET	Shipping will be U.P.S. in the states, unless otherwise arranged. Out of country buyers should inquire for shipping charges	_____ **@ $3.50 =** _______

TOTAL CHECK ENCLOSED: $ _______________

Photocopy, fill out, and send with your check to:

VITREOUS GROUP/CAMP COLTON
CAMP COLTON
COLTON, OR 97017
(503) 824-3150